Hope IGNITED

Set Free from the Grip of Anxiety & Depression

Maria I. Morgan

Published by hope*books
2217 Matthews Township Pkwy
Suite D302
Matthews, NC 28105
www.hopebooks.com

hope*books is a division of hope*media

Printed in the United States of America

First paperback edition.
Paperback ISBN: 979-8-89185-403-1
Hardcover ISBN: 979-8-89185-345-4
Ebook ISBN: 979-8-89185-397-3
Library of Congress Number: 2025950940

Scripture references are from The King James Version (KJV) and are in the public domain. They have been used with reverence for those who spent their lives translating the Word.

"As a pastor, I am deeply grateful for the ministry of Maria Morgan and her willingness to be open and transparent in sharing her story. *Hope Ignited* rises above many books in this field, weaving together biblical truth with practical application and speaking in a way that those who truly need hope can understand. This book points us to the God who restores and reminds us that with Him, hope is never lost."

—**Trent Cornwell**, Senior Pastor
Vision Baptist Church, Alpharetta, GA

"Maria Morgan's hope-filled story of healing from trauma and depression is one that only God could write. Through biblical truth and scientific facts, the author's journey to freedom will inspire you to believe Christ can— and will—deliver sufferers as they surrender to His care. Begin your venture to victory with this highly recommended book!"

—**Leslie Bennett**, Director of Women's Ministry
Initiatives, Revive Our Hearts

"Rarely does a book on these delicate subjects of the soul capture the proper balance of honest vulnerability and refreshing hope—this well-crafted work by Maria sweetly and bravely accomplishes just that. Its content goes beyond descriptive narratives of the long, intense shadows to include wonderfully prescriptive antidotes practically aligned with God's Spirit and undergirded with careful exposition of His Word. A must read for not only those who suffer in the throes of depression and anxiety but also all who yearn to better support and serve with constructive empathy those who do. I highly recommend it."

—Harley Snode, President/Biblical Counselor,
Inspire Counseling Ministries

"In *Hope Ignited*, Maria Morgan courageously shares her journey through the depths of anxiety, depression, and even suicidal despair, and in doing so, she offers readers a lifeline of encouragement and truth. With transparency, she weaves together personal testimony with biblical hope in a way that is both practical and compassionate. As a clinical neuropsychologist who knows the healing power of Christ, I can attest this book is a resource for anyone who feels trapped in the darkness or who longs to better support a loved one. Maria's story reminds us that no matter how heavy the burden, God is faithful to restore, renew, and redeem. This book will leave you not only comforted but encouraged to take the next step toward freedom."

—Dr. Michelle Bengtson, Clinical Neuropsychologist,
international speaker, podcast host, and author of
Hope Prevails: Insights from a Doctor's Personal Journey Through Depression, and *Breaking Anxiety's Grip*

"In Maria Morgan's powerful book, *Hope Ignited*, she courageously shares her downward spiral into deep depression, debilitating anxiety, and devastating psychosis. Thankfully, her story does not end there. Through God's amazing grace, love, and mercy, she found hope, healing, and freedom, and she wants to help others find it too.

Biblically grounded, filled with Scripture, and packed with fascinating scientific facts about how God created our bodies, *Hope Ignited* is a balm for the soul. Readers will find practical tips to live out the truth of God's Word, what it means to have a personal relationship with Jesus Christ, and how to become the healthy disciples God created them to be."

—**Doris Swift**, author of *Surrender the Joy Stealers: Rediscover the Jesus Joy in You*, speaker, and host of the *Fierce Calling* podcast

"*Hope Ignited* is tender, courageous, and theologically anchored—a rare blend of raw testimony, biblical truth, and practical, science-informed wisdom. As a licensed psychotherapist, I recognize the depth and integrity of Maria Morgan's approach. She names anxiety, depression, and even psychosis without shame, and then gently shows a way forward—body, soul, and spirit. I especially appreciate how she pairs Scripture with clear definitions, reflection questions, and doable steps, offering real help to both sufferers and the loved ones who walk beside them. This isn't platitude-level hope; it's the kind forged in dark valleys and held by the presence of Jesus. If you (or someone you love) are weary from the fight and wondering if freedom is possible, let this book take your hand and lead you toward it. I'm grateful for Maria's voice—and I highly recommend *Hope Ignited.*"

—**Dr. Zoe Shaw**, licensed psychotherapist, author of *Stronger in the Difficult Places*, and host of the *Stronger in the Difficult Places* podcast

"*Hope Ignited* is a bold account of God's power to bring healing from the depths of anxiety, depression, and trauma. With both transparency and biblical truth, Maria shares her journey in a way that offers comfort and clarity to those who are hurting and confused. Her words bring hope in God's faithfulness to meet us in our darkest valleys and lead us into freedom. I highly recommend *Hope Ignited* to anyone longing for emotional and spiritual healing."

—Cheryl Lutz, speaker, certified biblical counselor, and author of *Securely Held, Finding Significance and Security in the Shelter of God's Embrace*

"As a coach who has witnessed the impact of trauma and shame in so many women's lives, I am deeply grateful for Maria I. Morgan's courage in sharing her story. With unflinching honesty and vulnerability, she names the realities of anxiety, depression, suicidal despair, and psychosis—giving voice to struggles that too often remain hidden in silence and shame. Her bravery makes it safer for countless other women to come out of hiding and know they are not alone. *Hope Ignited: Set Free from the Grip of Anxiety & Depression* is a lifeline for women of faith in the grips of despair.

It helps us all grow in understanding trauma and its profound impact on women's health—mental, emotional, physical, and relational—so that safer, shame-free spaces can be cultivated in our churches and communities. Maria reminds us that healing is possible, not because the pain is ignored, but because it is witnessed and met with compassion. Her story is a testimony of hope, showing us what can happen when we are no longer hidden but held."

—**Kate Bartley**, Physical Therapist,
Women's Empowerment & Embodied Freedom Coach,
and Author of *The Good Girl Rx*

"The hope-filled, yet vulnerable, dive into the pit of depression and anxiety shared throughout the book is relatable and relevant. You will benefit emotionally, mentally, spiritually, and physically from all the practical helps and applications. As a licensed independent social worker in the mental health field, I strongly recommend this book because it's not only on point with current research and helps, but is pointedly a victory of overcoming the grip of anxiety and depression. This hope will permeate your mental health struggle as you read it."

—**Amy Menter**, LISW-S

"*Hope Ignited* is a powerful testimony of God's redeeming love breaking through the darkness. With honesty and courage, Maria shares her battle with anxiety, depression, and the wounds of trauma. Her story points us to the truth that no pit is too deep for God's healing hand. Through Scripture, science, and her own journey, she offers both practical wisdom and spiritual encouragement. This book is a reminder that the Lord still heals, restores, and sets us free. For anyone longing for hope and freedom, *Hope Ignited* will guide your heart back to the One who makes all things new."

—**Kim Mosiman**, Author, *Reflections of Joy*

"In *Hope Ignited: Set Free from the Grip of Anxiety & Depression*, Maria I. Morgan delivers a raw, vulnerable, and faith-filled account of her journey through anxiety, depression, psychosis, and attempts to end her life. Through every dark valley, she clung to the unshakable hope found in Jesus Christ—and now invites readers to discover that same hope for themselves. The beautiful, hope-filled message woven throughout *Hope Ignited* is clear: no matter the depth of our pain or the heaviness of our battle, healing, freedom, and lasting joy are possible through Jesus Christ. As someone who serves those struggling with addiction and mental health concerns, I have witnessed Maria's genuine love for hurting people. Her compassion is as real as the hope she offers. I wholeheartedly recommend *Hope Ignited* to anyone battling mental illness, as well as to their loved ones, mental health professionals, and clergy who seek to bring Christ-centered hope and help to those in need."

—**Dawn R. Ward**, founder of The Faith to Flourish, Certified Life and Addiction and Mental Health Coach, Author, *From Guilt to Grace: Hope and Healing for Christian Moms of Addicted Children*

"*Hope Ignited* is a powerful reminder that healing is not the end of the story but the beginning of deeper surrender to God. With raw honesty and steadfast faith, Maria shows how seasons of anxiety, fear, and brokenness can become sacred spaces where God meets us with His strength and goodness. Her testimony of miraculous healing shines as evidence that God still heals today. By weaving in her husband's perspective as a caretaker, Maria also offers readers a compassionate glimpse into the challenges and grace of walking alongside a loved one in pain. Each page is filled with practical wisdom and gentle encouragement, inviting readers to trust Jesus with their whole selves—body, soul, and spirit. For anyone longing for renewed faith, lasting transformation, and the courage to share their own story, *Hope Ignited* will meet you right where you are and lead you toward true freedom in Christ."

—**Lea Turner**, speaker, coach, author of *The Freedom to Feel*, and co-founder of Writer-2-Writer

"*Hope Ignited* is a powerful and deeply vulnerable testimony of God's healing grace. With honesty and courage, Maria Morgan shares her journey of anxiety, depression, and psychosis, while pointing us to the One who restores body, soul, and spirit. Through her personal story, biblical truth, and practical wisdom, this book offers a lifeline of hope to anyone who feels trapped in despair. As a survivor of a failed suicide attempt, I personally resonate deeply with Maria's fear and disillusionment. As a believer in Jesus Christ, I know the freedom that He alone brings. *Hope Ignited* reminds us that even the darkest seasons can become a testimony to God's glory. This book is an invitation for the reader to experience the same freedom in Christ."

—**Susan Panzica**, Speaker, Author, Advocate

"I've had the privilege of knowing Maria before and after her psychosis, testify to her integrity and authenticity, and admire her deep love for Christ and others. I'm convinced it is that love that motivated her to courageously share her story. What a journey she and her family have been on! While I recognize God responds to each of us differently, healing some miraculously, others through medication and therapy, and still others when they pass from this present earth and into eternity, her experiences remind us of His tender heart for each of us and His desire to bring us increased wholeness. May her story encourage you to pursue the One who is always pursuing you."

—**Jennifer Slattery**, cohost of the *Faith Over Fear* podcast, and Friday host of the *Your Daily Bible Verse* podcast

Note to the Reader

As you journey through these pages, you'll encounter words such as *anxiety, depression,* and *psychosis.* To keep this book as clear as possible, I've included a brief definition the first time each of these words appears. For a fuller explanation, see *Appendix A: Understanding the Terms.*

In addition, to keep the text clean, citations for sources appear at the end of each chapter. My prayer is that this resource will serve you well, giving you understanding without distraction, so you can focus on the hope and encouragement God has for you.

To my beloved husband, Steven.

Thank you for living out the vow to walk

"in sickness and in health"

with such grace and devotion.

Your steadfast love and unshakable faith in Jesus

reflected the One who carried me through

my darkest valleys.

All glory and praise to Him.

Acknowledgments

I'm grateful to each person who has been part of making this book possible. It has been a team effort. Special thanks to:

My Lord and Savior, Jesus Christ—Thank You for sparing my life so I can share Your message of hope, forgiveness, and unconditional love. You have taken what the enemy meant for evil and turned it into something for my good and Your glory. I praise You for being the God who gives beauty for ashes (Isaiah 61:3). All praise and honor are Yours, my Abba Father.

My Husband—Steve, even in the middle of my deepest depression, you never lost hope that the Lord would use our journey in a redemptive way. You told me I would write a book. Thank you for showing me what unconditional love looks like—and for believing in me when I lacked hope. You are the love of my life and best friend, and I'm so thankful for you.

My Family—Riley and Josh, thank you for supporting Dad and me during this struggle. Thank you for your willingness to be there and listen no matter what. I love you both so much.

My Mom—Thank you for believing in me and always encouraging me to take one day at a time, even when I was at my lowest. You are precious to me and an inspiration. I love you.

My Brother—Karl, thank you for listening and talking with me during some of the most difficult times. Your commitment to help did not go unnoticed. I love you.

Prayer Team—Your prayers sustained me throughout this journey. Thank you for consistently bringing me and this book-writing process to the throne of grace. The Lord hears and answers prayer, and I'm thankful for each of you: Kathy Carnahan, Jessica Edwards, Ginger Haney, Patricia Huffman, Darlene King, Amy Menter, Holly Pearson, Sandy Pearson, Shannon Penrod, Rebecca Pepperdine, Marsha Stamas, Gina Widholm, Rhonda Wilson, and Eileen Wipf.

Vision Baptist Church—Your unconditional love, prayers, and support during our struggle and beyond will never be forgotten. Thank you for ministering to us during the trial and for giving us the opportunity to share all that God has done since then. We're especially thankful for the staff: Senior Pastor Trent Cornwell, Administrative Pastor Beau Carpenter, and Family Ministry Director Gregory Keelen

hope*books (Brian Dixon and Team)—Thank you for believing in me and in the importance of sharing my hope story. Your step-by-step support and guidance have provided the framework I needed to launch this book into the world. The friendships I've made in this community are priceless.

Beta Readers—Thank you for dedicating your time to reading my manuscript in its rough stages. Every comment and suggestion throughout the process has strengthened the book and made it more relevant to readers. I'm grateful for you: Pastor Trent Cornwell, Rhonda Gibby, Bonnie McDonald, Amy Menter, Kim Mosiman, Lea Turner, Holly Pearson, Gina Widholm, and Brandy Williamson.

Writer-2-Writer—Special thanks to Kim Mosiman and Lea Turner for helping me navigate the launch process. I appreciate your hard work and dedication to making the entire experience enjoyable.

Contents

Foreword

*T*hank you for prioritizing your physical, mental, and spiritual health. It matters more than you may realize. If you're holding this book in your hands, it's likely because you're walking through a difficult season. I want you to know, you are not alone. I've experienced incredibly dark valleys, too.

Before we continue, I want to be upfront about something important. My story touches on anxiety, depression, psychosis, and the painful reality of suicide. If you're in a vulnerable place, please make sure you're in a safe and supportive environment as you read. If you're struggling with suicidal thoughts, I urge you to reach out to the 988 Suicide & Crisis Lifeline. It's available twenty-four hours a day, seven days a week for support and assistance.[1] You are priceless, and your life matters.

Because words like *anxiety*, *depression*, and *psychosis* can feel heavy or unclear, let me briefly share what I mean when I use them in this book. *Anxiety* is that ongoing weight of fear and worry, often accompanied by physical symptoms. *Depression* is the deep, lingering sadness and loss of interest that touches every part of life. *Psychosis* is an altered state where reality becomes distorted by delusions or hallucinations.

When anxiety and depression weigh heavily, our thoughts often become unreliable. In those moments, it's easy to forget the truth: you are loved, needed, and created with a purpose. Even when you can't feel it—especially then—hold on to the promise that God has a plan for your life and that He's not finished writing your story.

Being in the valley is a sobering experience, often marked by hardship and uncertainty. It's an uncomfortable place that can push us to our limits. When I found myself in the depths of depression, after two suicide attempts and nine months of psychosis, my only focus was escaping the pain. Maybe you can relate. If you're in that barren place now, desperately searching for a way out and coming up empty, please don't give up. Hold on. There is hope.

Seek the Lord, and invite a trusted, biblically grounded counselor or advisor to walk with you. Stay open and take the next right step. Don't rush the process. Allow the Lord to set the pace.

Consider two short verses from the book of James to encourage your heart: "My brethren, count it all joy when ye fall into divers temptations; Knowing this, that the trying of your faith worketh patience" (James 1:2–3).

What takeaways can we find in these two brief verses? First, trials are universal—every believer faces them, including you and me. Second, we're invited to embrace these trials with joy. Not because the trials themselves are pleasant, but because we trust the Lord to bring about something good through them. Finally, don't miss this beautiful truth: as we endure trials with our eyes fixed on Jesus, He develops patience within us.

Patience is the ability to accept or tolerate delay, trouble, or suffering without becoming agitated or upset.[2] It's so much more than waiting. Patient endurance prepares us to face future trials with resilience because we've learned to trust the One who walks with us through each storm.

There is no denying it: life is hard, and the struggle you're facing is real. But those twenty-two words from the book of James offer you a reason to take another breath, lift your eyes, and look to the One who holds your future. Every trial has a purpose—to make us look more like our Savior, Jesus Christ. Choose to take a step forward in faith.

By God's grace, my life is proof that healing is possible. Medical professionals have told me it's rare for someone to recover from the advanced psychosis I endured. Though I still have to guard against thought patterns that can lead to anxiety and depression, I continue to grow each day, applying the lessons the Lord is teaching me.

It's no surprise that the Lord often works through our weaknesses, transforming our trials into testimonies. My intense struggle with anxiety and depression didn't just end in healing—it sparked a deep passion for helping other women, like you, find freedom, joy, and purpose.

I love the way Paul says it: "Blessed be God, even the Father of our Lord Jesus Christ, the Father of mercies, and the God of all comfort; Who comforteth us in all our tribulation, that we may be able to comfort them which are in any trouble, by the comfort wherewith we ourselves are comforted of God" (2 Corinthians 1:3–4).

Although our stories may be very different, it is an honor and a privilege to come alongside you on this journey, offering practical help that points you to the One who is the God of all comfort. The Lord, who renewed my trust and ignited hope in my life, is willing and able to do the same for you. With our God, what seems impossible becomes possible. We have His promise: "For with God nothing shall be impossible" (Luke 1:37). I'd love to pray for you.

> *Heavenly Father, Thank You for who You are. You are holy and righteous, gracious and kind, full of love and compassion. You are good, and You always do what is right. Your mercies are new every morning, and Your faithfulness is great. Thank you for inviting us to come boldly before Your throne to find mercy and grace in our time of need. And we need it today. I lift up my friend who is struggling with anxiety, depression, or even suicidal thoughts. You see her. You know her. She is Your child. You love her with an everlasting love. Help her grasp Your love and to know she matters to You. Assure her that You will never leave or forsake her. She is never alone. Fill her with Your peace as she leans on You. Use Your Word to light her path. Show her the next step to take today. Let Your peace, which passes all understanding, guard and keep her heart and mind through Christ Jesus. Thank You in advance for meeting each of her needs. In the mighty name of Jesus, the One who heals all our diseases, Amen.*

Works Cited

[1]   "NAMI Helpline." *National Alliance on Mental Illness*, https://www.nami.org/support-education/nami-helpline. Accessed 21 Apr. 2025.

[2]   "Patience." *Merriam-Webster.com Dictionary*, https://www.merriam-webster.com/dictionary/patience. Accessed 21 Apr. 2025.

How Did I Get Here?

*A*nxiety gripped me like an unwelcome guest that refused to leave. It was late 2020, and the feelings were unmistakable. It wasn't the first time I'd faced it. Fifteen years earlier, while in my late thirties, anxiety crept in after a traumatic car accident. But this time was different. There was no car accident, no apparent trigger. And yet, the same paralyzing fear had returned. I didn't understand what was happening.

In the final months of 2020, my husband, Steve, and I stepped into the role of caregivers for my mother-in-law. She had dementia, and it was a privilege to honor her during a difficult season in her life. But at times, she was insistent on doing things that weren't safe, sparking tense discussions between her and Steve. The ongoing conflict from those arguments became overwhelming for me. At the time, I didn't understand why, but conflict would become a key to unlocking something more profound, something we'll explore in Chapter 4.

When those three months ended, we dropped my mother-in-law off at Steve's sister's house in South Carolina. As we drove away, I expected the anxiety to lift and relief to take its place. Instead, the anxious thoughts and a deep sense of dread settled even more deeply into my heart. *Had I done something wrong? Was God angry with me?* I wanted to escape the storm brewing inside and return to some sense of normalcy.

Determined to move forward, I threw myself back into the activities I had paused during her stay: co-leading a prayer team, teaching a middle school Life Group with Steve, and facilitating an online study of Shannon Popkin's book, *Comparison Girl: Lessons from Jesus on Me-Free Living in a Measure-Up World.*[1]

Unhealthy Thoughts

While grappling with anxiety during the book study, I found myself reading each chapter through a distorted lens, convinced I was guilty of exactly what the author warned against: comparing myself to other women in ministry, wealth, looks, status, and more. My thoughts spiraled: *If I'm comparing myself in all these areas, I certainly shouldn't be facilitating this study. I don't have my act together. I don't measure up. I'm not worthy to be leading.*

Unaware of how unhealthy my thinking had become, the enemy had me firmly in his grip, caught in a tailspin of self-doubt. Distorted thoughts clamored for my attention until I made a choice: step down from the study and stop teaching. For the first time in my life, I didn't finish what I started. I quit.

Throughout 2021, I slowly disengaged from all ministry-related work. Truthfully, I struggled just to read my Bible. In my anxious, depressed state, all I could see on the pages of Scripture was condemnation.

Interacting with friends and family became increasingly difficult. Even communication with my husband grew strained. I isolated myself, trapped in the destructive thought patterns swirling in my mind. I felt distant from God and completely alone.

The Initial Spiral

Both times I experienced severe anxiety, in 2006 and again in 2021, the physical symptoms were identical: insomnia and weight loss, accompanied by shallow breathing, a rapid heart rate, and a tingling sensation throughout my body. Now in my mid-fifties, I found myself stuck in the same overwhelming cycle.

The first bout of anxiety was triggered by a car accident. While making a left turn, I was struck on the driver's side by a vehicle attempting to pass in a no-passing zone. Fortunately, my physical injuries were minimal, soft tissue damage in my neck, as well as ribs that were partially dislocated.

But when the attending officer assigned me thirty percent of the blame, the unjust accusation shook me. *How could I be at fault when the other driver had broken the law?* I was caught in the grip of conflict beyond my control.

Over the next few weeks, lack of sleep and an allergic reaction to the prescribed pain medication deepened my spiral into severe anxiety. With the support of family, friends, doctors, and a Christian counselor, I fully recovered within nine months.

The Battle Returns

Though I had won my first battle with anxiety, its return in 2021 caught me off guard. I recognized the familiar, debilitating pattern. As weeks turned into months, depression settled in, just as it had before—an unwelcome but well-documented reality for 20 to 70 percent of those struggling with anxiety disorders.[2] I was sinking into a dark place, losing hope, and the will to go on.

Despite countless doctor visits and regular counseling, I was worn down physically, mentally, and emotionally. Instead of improving, my condition continued to worsen. By November 2021, I reached a breaking point. I attempted to take my life with my husband's prescription medication. Emergency room staff stabilized me before transferring me to the first behavioral health facility with an available bed.

The state-mandated stay only deepened my distress. Everything blended into an exhausting routine. As the nights dragged on without rest, sleep deprivation began to take its toll. Auditory hallucinations (voices and phantom sounds) grew more frequent. My blood pressure and blood sugar spiked. My appetite disappeared. The mandatory group meetings, meant to help, only heightened my anxiety. I dreaded what staff and patients might be thinking.

The Weight of Guilt and Shame

When Steve brought me home several days later, guilt and shame consumed me. How could my husband still love me after what I had done? I agonized over the impact on our daughter and son-in-law. No doubt, my mom and brother were devastated. I was convinced God was angry with me. I saw no end to the widening ripples created by my impulsive decision.

More than anything, I wanted to erase the haunting memories—my suicide attempt, the week-long stay at the psychiatric facility—and pretend life was as it had been before anxiety took hold.

Reengaging in normal activities was challenging. Returning to church felt particularly uncomfortable. As a former teacher and leader, I was mortified by the thought of what others might think of me. I kept conversations brief and superficial, avoiding genuine connection. Instead of taking my thoughts captive to the obedience of Christ, I allowed them to run wild (2 Corinthians 10:5). Over time, I convinced myself I had no friends, never realizing I was the one who had severed every connection.

Behind the Mask

Despite everything, Steve forgave me completely, welcoming me home and assuring me of his unconditional love. Recognizing my ongoing need for help and support, he enrolled me in a highly acclaimed ten-week intensive outpatient program.

Even after completing the program and undergoing months of counseling, I experienced little, if any, improvement. But I hid my feelings and continued to pretend the treatment was helping. All the while, I avoided ministry. I kept my distance from others, fearing they would see the mess inside of me. Clinging desperately to the image I believed others saw, I became my own worst enemy: trapped in a cycle of hopelessness and despair.

Nearly a year had passed since my first attempt, and by November 2022, I couldn't pretend any longer. Steve was away on a trip, and the weather turned stormy. Sleep-deprived and struggling, I took our potty-training puppy outside. With the rain pouring down in sheets, she refused to go to the bathroom.

Drenched, infuriated, and powerless to control the situation, it became the final straw. I felt the weight of my depression crashing down on me. I just wanted the mental anguish to end.

That afternoon, I took a massive overdose of my prescription medication. It was a dangerous mix of psychiatric drugs and painkillers. Violent tremors shook my body as I faded in and out of consciousness. Yet, in God's boundless grace, He preserved my life once again.

Reality Unravels

Not long afterward, psychosis took hold. Days and nights blurred into a haze of irrational thoughts. Paranoia and suspicion warped my perception. I became consumed by the belief that Steve would either divorce me or eliminate me for what I had done. I was hesitant to voice my suspicions. Fear kept me silent. If he genuinely was trying to harm me, revealing my thoughts might only confirm his intentions.

Driven by desperation, I would listen in on his phone calls and research for hours, convinced he had set up electromagnetic fields, hidden surveillance cameras, and deliberately introduced mold into our home to harm me. When I found batteries and metal objects in our junk drawers, it felt like confirmation. Finding mold in the ductwork and on the fabric of a nearby couch only reinforced my fears.

Steve humored me, emptying the junk drawers and letting me clean the moldy areas, but my suspicions didn't waver. Even his extended leave from work and desperate search for doctors to help me didn't shift my thinking. I was gripped by the belief he was working with them against me.

Steve reached out to key family members. Our daughter and son-in-law, my mom, and my brother all knew about the severity of my illness. When I refused to follow the doctor's instructions or listen to reason, he had me speak with one of them, hoping their words might help. Instead, my suspicions soon spread beyond Steve and the medical team, distorting my view of family and friends until I no longer trusted anyone.

The War Within

I firmly believed everyone was plotting against me, including those who had been most supportive. For nine grueling months, I existed in a relentless state of fight or flight.

A deep-seated anger simmered just beneath the surface. My volatile emotions alarmed me. Like a cornered animal, I felt trapped, lashing out at my husband in a frantic attempt to protect myself. Yet despite the verbal assaults, I was overwhelmed by the fear of losing him. I was terrified to be alone.

By this time, I could no longer reconcile my actions with those of a child of God. *Christ-followers wouldn't struggle with these things, would they?*

The remorse was suffocating. Ending my life had never seemed like an option, yet here I was, crushed under the weight of two failed suicide attempts. *How had I reached this place of hopelessness?* I didn't understand.

Drowning in guilt and shame, not only for my two suicide attempts, but for the person I had become, I believed the enemy's lies: I was unsaved, beyond redemption. In my distorted thinking, there was only one conclusion—hell was my final destination. As powerful as my previous desire had been to end it all, the horrifying reality of eternal torment gave me a desperate will to live.

The Turning Point

By mid-August 2023, after months of burying my thoughts and fears, the tension that had been building finally erupted. I hadn't been honest with my husband, family, psychologist, or psychiatrist, too afraid they'd hospitalize me or send me to a residential care facility. One evening, a simple question from my husband triggered an outburst. Hours of pent-up emotion came spilling out in the form of accusations. I was sure he wanted to end our marriage, or worse, remove me from his life completely.

Steve couldn't believe what he was hearing. After two and a half years of standing by me through therapy sessions and doctor visits, it felt like we were back at square one. But he didn't give up. Determined to intervene, Steve documented the irrational beliefs I had shared and made a plan. The next day, Saturday, August 12, he invited several people to come over: our pastor, his wife, and four couples from church who had faithfully walked with us through our struggles. He wanted them to speak the truth, offer prayer, and remind me of God's love.

I dreaded the day, convinced it was part of some larger scheme to get rid of me. But when I finally opened up, confessing what I had done and voicing the fears that haunted me, something unexpected happened. Instead of judgment or rejection, I was met with love. Unconditional love. It was one of the hardest things I'd ever done, and yet, one of the most healing. My vulnerability was received with grace, and in that beautiful exchange, the door to my mind cracked open. I saw just a glimmer of light—hope.

More Light

Throughout my mental and emotional battle, Steve remained a pillar of support and truth. I can't thank him enough for living out the vow to stand beside me "in sickness and in health."

The Lord gave him incredible wisdom and insight. God also used Steve in practical ways. He carefully organized my irrational thoughts into specific categories, assigning them to the women who had gathered with us on what we now call *The Day of Truth*. It was my responsibility to follow up with them each week, sharing the truth about my progress.

Two weeks later, one of the women invited me to her house. She was preparing a lesson for our upcoming ladies' meeting. It was the group she'd encouraged me to attend many times before, though I always found a reason to avoid it. Her topic? *Redemption.*

Once again, I was confronted with a concept I knew well, but because of my suicide attempts, I had struggled to embrace it. As I left my friend's home, I carried a powerful reminder with me: *There is no sin too great for God to forgive.* She encouraged me to attend the meeting that Friday, and for the first time that year, I said yes. The door to my mind opened a bit wider.

The next day, I reached out to a long-time friend and opened up, sharing a glimpse of my story. I recounted the pain I had carried for the last couple of years. Her response caught my attention. She mentioned a pastor friend who had written a book about suicide. As soon as I hung up, I searched for the book on Amazon, expanding my search to "suicide and the Christian." I was stunned by the number of titles that filled the screen. In that moment, something clicked. I realized other believers had also walked this road. The sliver of hope grew brighter. The door to my mind was now more than halfway open.

Truth That Makes You Free

On Friday, September 1, 2023, I attended the ladies' event at church. A friend, who had faithfully sent cards during some of my lowest moments, started talking to me before the meeting began. As she shared some of the things she was going through, I was stunned to hear thought patterns that mirrored my own. She had no idea what I had been battling, but God used her transparency to show me something profound: *I wasn't alone.* The door to my mind was now wide open, and light flooded in.

After the meeting, I sat in my Jeep, holding the list of irrational beliefs Steve had compiled. Everything from the past three weeks—*The Day of Truth*, the lesson on redemption, the book recommendation, the friend's struggle—had been orchestrated by God. They were all leading me here. I was at a crossroads: *should I continue striving to handle life on my own, or surrender fully and trust the Lord?* After years of trying to control every detail around me, I was physically and emotionally drained. The choice was clear: *I trust You, Lord! I no longer want to live by these irrational beliefs. I want to be free.*

As I spoke the words aloud, something broke. The Lord instantly lifted the lingering weight of anxiety and depression. The chains of fear and doubt shattered. A dam of tension burst, releasing everything that had been trapped inside for so long. Tears flowed as I lifted my hands in surrender. My heart was filled with peace. For the first time in years, nothing stood between me and my Savior. When I opened my hands in surrender, the Lord brought healing.

Only God!

During my struggle, and in the early days that followed, Steve prayed earnestly. The Lord gave him insight into the true source of my anxiety: unhealed wounds from childhood that had planted seeds of fear and mistrust. Growing up with an alcoholic father whose words and actions created conflict, I learned to shut down during his angry outbursts, desperate to avoid becoming the target of his rage.

Even as an adult, when Steve's mom was staying with us and I witnessed them arguing, I felt like that little girl again—helpless and unable to control the chaos around me. I hadn't realized it, but I was projecting the mistrust I felt toward my dad onto my husband, and even onto God.

But God. Through the unwavering love of my husband, the fervent prayers and fasting of friends and family, and the tender mercy of my gracious Heavenly Father, something miraculous happened.

God redeemed what the enemy meant for evil, restoring my joy, hope, and purpose. If He did it for me, He can do it for you too.

Works Cited

[1] Popkin, Shannon. *Comparison Girl: Lessons from Jesus on Me-Free Living in a Measure-Up World.* Kregel Publications, 2020.

[2] Giorgi, Anna. "Anxiety and Depression Overlap: Link Between Comorbid Disorders." *Verywell Health*, 6 Feb. 2024, https://www.verywellhealth.com/anxiety-and-depression-8547945. Accessed 21 May 2025.

Part 1:
Your Body

1

Your Body Is Telling You Something

My Life Lesson

I remember the night my body finally gave in to the physical symptoms of anxiety. It had been an ordinary day, but as I lay down to sleep, an odd sensation jolted me awake. It was sharp, startling, almost like an electrical shock. I had felt this once before, fifteen years earlier, during my first struggle with anxiety.

Looking back, I missed the subtle warning signs: rapid heartbeat, shallow breathing, muscle tension, and fatigue. I didn't realize what they were. Instead, I kept searching for a specific event to explain what had happened, but there wasn't one.

The Slow Build-Up

The truth? It wasn't a single event. Stress had been building steadily for months. My husband, Steve, and I were navigating the challenges of the COVID-19 pandemic while also caring for his mother. Just days after his sister stepped in as caregiver, Steve underwent rotator cuff surgery. Complications followed, requiring an unexpected trip to the emergency room and months of physical therapy. My once-optimistic outlook began to fade.

The pressure was mounting, and my body couldn't keep up. As my stress responses went unchecked, they slowly escalated into full-blown anxiety. My thoughts spiraled out of control like a runaway train, and I became fixated on every physical symptom. I researched endlessly and feared the worst.

The more I focused on how I felt, the worse everything became. I wrestled with sleepless nights, digestive issues, and overwhelming fatigue. Each morning, the simplest tasks, such as showering, getting ready, and preparing meals, felt impossible. All I wanted was to lie down and shut everything out.

Life in Survival Mode

The lack of sleep had a negative impact, not only on my body but also on my ability to process information. Things that once came easily now felt monumental. Preparing a simple thirty-minute meal stretched into an hour. I'd gather ingredients, only to forget what I needed. I had to reread the instructions repeatedly to be sure I didn't miss a step. It was as if my brain had shifted into low gear, and I couldn't get it back in drive.

Cleaning the house was just as challenging. My thoughts felt disjointed. I'd walk back and forth, trying to remember what supplies I needed to clean the bathrooms. Even the simplest chores drained what little energy I had left.

Before anxiety and depression took hold of my life, I had been committed to regular exercise. Fitness walking and weight training were part of my routine. But in that season, conserving energy became my top priority. Without restorative sleep, my mind was foggy, my body couldn't recover, and eventually, I gave up on exercising altogether.

Shortly after insomnia started, I began battling digestive issues. Every time I ate, I experienced stomach pain, followed by diarrhea. Food lost its appeal, and planning meals felt too demanding. I quickly began losing weight. This same pattern mirrored what I had experienced years earlier when battling anxiety and depression. It was a relentless cycle—one that undermined my confidence, leaving me feeling weak and fragile.

Hitting Rock Bottom

Months of fitful sleep and poor nutrition made it difficult for my body to function the way it once had. Despite Steve's consistent encouragement to eat well, stay active, and get proper rest, nothing seemed to make a difference. In my anxious state, I felt things had already spiraled too far out of control to be reversed. Distorted thinking played a significant role in the decline of my health.

For two and a half years, exhaustion clouded my ability to make decisions. Each suicide attempt came from a place of utter weariness, when the weight of pain seemed impossible to carry any longer. I just wanted it all to end.

The exhaustion was real and only compounded my physical issues. But what I didn't realize at the time was that the pain ran deeper. It was primarily emotional.

After the second suicide attempt, I hit rock bottom. Psychosis set in, an altered state where I lost touch with reality (see Appendix A). Steve was deeply distressed and unsure of what to do next. His boss approved a five-week leave of absence, allowing Steve to consult with every doctor who might offer insight: general practitioners, neurologists, and dietitians.

Losing Touch with Reality

When my primary care physician ran bloodwork, she discovered I was prediabetic and recommended medication, but in my psychotic state, I refused to consider it. Soon after, my neurologist diagnosed me with dangerously low levels of vitamin B12 and vitamin D3, and prescribed corrective shots, advice I chose to ignore.

Still, plagued by joint pain and extreme fatigue, I spent hours scouring the internet for conditions that matched my symptoms. Around this time, I also abandoned the vitamin supplements I had relied on for years: women's multivitamins, calcium, magnesium, and vitamin C and vitamin D. In my delusion, I even removed the hormone patch I had been prescribed years earlier after my hysterectomy, sure it was harming me. That decision only made things worse: my mood swings intensified, brain fog deepened, and my joints and muscles ached.

During the nine months I was in psychosis, I became convinced my food and water were being poisoned. Fearing

I had multiple allergies, I restricted my diet to just a handful of items: eggs, chicken, fish, apples, and biscuits. During those months, my weight fluctuated by twenty pounds—a visible sign of my inner struggle.

A Wake-Up Call

My visit to the dietitian was a wake-up call. She pointed out a variety of foods I could incorporate into my meals, encouraging me to eat several small meals a day, and emphasizing the importance of tracking my calorie intake. Until then, even the thought of keeping up with calories had felt overwhelming. But to gain weight, I needed to consume more calories than my body was using.

I'd been content with my weight before spiraling into anxiety and depression. Losing so much made me self-conscious all over again, stirring up the old stigma of being underweight as a teenager. Now, as an adult, I was painfully aware that my clothes no longer fit. I was sure everyone else noticed, too.

Reluctantly, I began following my dietitian's guidelines and monitoring my calories. Little by little, I started to gain weight. I added an extra meal to my routine, but focused more on calorie count than nourishment, reaching for fried foods loaded with carbohydrates. Over time, these unhealthy choices disrupted my gut health, depleted nutrients, and caused my blood sugar to fluctuate wildly.

Looking back, it's clear that anxiety and depression had wreaked havoc on my physical health. I carried stress at the soul level that affected every part of my body. As my health declined, my thoughts spiraled downward, further weakening my body.

But here's the good news: God designed our bodies to be resilient. The effects of anxiety and depression don't have to be permanent. I've seen this firsthand. When we break the cycle and reintroduce healthy practices into our lives, our bodies can recover, just as mine has.

My experience isn't unique, and there's solid science that helps explain why.

The Science Behind It

Our Creator didn't overlook a single detail when He made us. His design is both intricate and awe-inspiring. Consider a few of the "ingredients" He included in our physical design:

- **Genetic code and DNA**
- **Musculoskeletal system**
- **Cardiovascular system**
- **Respiratory system**
- **Sensory systems**
- **Reproductive system**
- **Immune system**

Each system has a specific role, yet all work together in harmony, enabling us to grow, adapt, and thrive. But when sin entered the world after the Fall, our bodies became subject to sickness, disease, and eventually, death.

Even with its limitations, the human body reflects an astonishing level of intelligence and design. It sends us early warning signs when something isn't working as it should:

pain, inflammation, fatigue, digestive issues, skin changes, mental and emotional symptoms, respiratory symptoms, cardiovascular symptoms, neurological symptoms, and even loss of function. Like the check-engine light in a car, these red flags signal it's time to pay attention and get things checked out.

When Stress Becomes Anxiety

Stress is a natural, God-given response to threats or challenges we face every day. It helps us stay alert, focused, and motivated.[1] But when the stress response becomes chronic, when our bodies are constantly flooded with hormones like cortisol and adrenaline, it starts to work against us.[2] That's when stress can evolve into anxiety.

Unlike stress, which is often tied to a specific cause, anxiety tends to linger. It spreads quietly, affecting every part of daily life. Anxiety can be harder to manage because it's not always easy to trace.

How Anxiety Affects the Body and Mind

How does anxiety affect our bodies? We might experience high blood pressure, muscle tension, frequent headaches, or a racing heart. Over time, these physical symptoms are joined by mental and emotional ones: restlessness, persistent worry, difficulty concentrating, and an ongoing sense of being overwhelmed.[3]

The Role of Holistic Health

Many interconnected factors contribute to our physical health:

- **Sleep**
- **Nutrition**

- **Exercise**
- **Genetics**
- **Preventive care**
- **Environmental factors**
- **Social and community support**
- **Mental health**
- **Spiritual health**

When any one of these foundational components—like sleep, nutrition, or exercise—is lacking, our overall health begins to suffer. Anxiety often disrupts several of these areas at once, compounding its effects and making recovery more difficult.

The Impact of Missing the Basics

Over time, the body's ability to heal, maintain energy, and function well becomes impaired:

- **Sleep deprivation:** Without enough sleep, physical performance declines, and the risk of accidents increases. Sleep is essential for repair and restoration. Without it, the immune system becomes more vulnerable, making it easier for illness to develop. Our brains also struggle to function well, which can affect memory, concentration, and mood regulation. Over time, chronic sleep deprivation is linked to serious health issues, including high blood pressure, diabetes, obesity, and even dementia.[4]

- **Poor nutrition:** When our diets lack key nutrients, our bodies can't perform at their best. We feel drained, sluggish, and more susceptible to illness. Deficiencies in vitamins and minerals can lead to hormonal imbalances, weakened bones, fatigue, and a compromised immune system. Over time, poor eating habits may result in obesity, heart disease, and diabetes.[5]

- **Lack of exercise:** When we stop moving regularly, we miss out on many benefits of physical activity, including a healthier heart, stronger muscles, increased energy, and improved mental clarity. A sedentary lifestyle also raises the risk of obesity, muscle atrophy, cardiovascular issues, and chronic diseases like type 2 diabetes and some cancers.[6]

When It All Adds Up

Do you notice a pattern? Prolonged anxiety and depression don't just affect the mind; they take a serious toll on the body, increasing the risk of obesity, diabetes, and heart disease.

All three of these lifestyle factors—sleep deprivation, poor nutrition, and lack of exercise—played a role in my physical decline. Have you noticed similar patterns in your life? If so, here are a few small steps you can take to begin improving your overall health:

- **Prioritize sleep:** Set a consistent bedtime, create a calming nighttime routine, and limit screen time before bed. These simple adjustments can help your body rest and begin to heal.

- **Improve nutrition:** Include more fruits, vegetables, lean proteins, and whole grains in your meals. You may be surprised by how quickly good nutrition lifts your energy and mood.

- **Start moving:** Begin slowly by aiming for thirty

minutes of moderate exercise most days. Choose an activity you enjoy: walking, biking, or swimming. Strength training can also be a powerful tool for managing anxiety and depression.

God designed our bodies with purpose and wisdom. When we understand how anxiety and depression affect us physically, and start making small, intentional changes, we can take a meaningful step toward healing.

While science helps explain what's happening in our bodies, God's Word offers the deepest source of comfort and lasting hope.

Help and Hope from God's Word

Our Heavenly Father designed us to be unique, distinct from everything else He created. The book of Genesis offers us front-row seats to the creation of the first humans, Adam and Eve:

> And the Lord God formed man of the dust of the ground, and breathed into his nostrils the breath of life; and man became a living soul...
>
> And the Lord God caused a deep sleep to fall upon Adam, and he slept: and he took one of his ribs, and closed up the flesh instead thereof; And the rib, which the Lord God had taken from man, made he a woman, and brought her unto the man.
>
> —Genesis 2:7, 21–22

Created from the Elements

Our physical bodies were created from dust, the basic elements of the earth. God gathered these nutrients together to form Adam's body, crafting every detail with divine intention.

Even the tiniest particles in the soil whisper of God's creativity and care. Here are some of the key elements God used in forming the human body:

- **Carbon (C):** forms the backbone of all organic life: proteins, carbohydrates, fats, and nucleic acids (DNA and RNA)
- **Hydrogen (H):** essential for water and energy within the body
- **Oxygen (O):** fuels cellular respiration and energy production
- **Nitrogen (N):** builds proteins and genetic material
- **Phosphorus (P):** strengthens bones, powers energy transfer (ATP), and supports cell function
- **Potassium (K):** regulates heartbeat, nerves, and muscle contraction
- **Calcium (Ca):** needed for bone strength and cellular communication
- **Sulfur (S):** aids in detoxification and protein formation
- **Magnesium (Mg):** supports muscle function and energy metabolism
- **Trace elements (Fe, Zn, Cu, I):** support immunity, healing, oxygen transport, and hormone balance[7]

Although proteins and vitamins aren't fully formed in soil, the essential elements and compounds required for their creation are present. Think of the soil as God's toolkit, providing all the building blocks we need for life.

Crafted by God's Hands

Picture the God of the universe stooping down to create man's body. Unlike the rest of His handiwork, which He brought into existence with His spoken word, man was crafted by God's very own hands.

Once God gathered the dust that contained all the necessary nutrients, He breathed into man's nostrils the breath of life. Man became a living soul, made in the image of His Creator. Humanity is the climax of God's creative work, the grand finale of all He accomplished in six days: "And God saw every thing that he had made, and, behold, it was very good. And the evening and the morning were the sixth day" (Genesis 1:31).

God didn't create us by accident. He formed us with intention and for a divine purpose. He created male and female to bring glory to Himself and to display the gospel of Jesus Christ. Both Adam and Eve were designed to worship God. Can you imagine them walking with Him each day, excited to see Him, share all that was happening, and listen to His loving voice?

When Sin Entered the Story

Sin broke Adam and Eve's fellowship with God and changed everything. Not only did it bring devastating spiritual consequences, but it also introduced mental and physical suffering, pain, sorrow, and ultimately death. As Genesis 3:19

puts it: "In the sweat of thy face shalt thou eat bread, till thou return unto the ground; for out of it wast thou taken: for dust thou art, and unto dust shalt thou return."

Since the Fall, sickness has become a reality in our lives. The Old and New Testaments offer numerous examples of people plagued by illness. Remember the woman who suffered from a bleeding disorder for twelve long years? She spent all she had seeking help from countless doctors, yet none could heal her. Instead, her condition only grew worse.

When she heard that Jesus was in her town, she was determined to reach Him, despite the crowd. Her motivation? She believed that if she could just touch His clothes, she would experience healing. Notice Christ's response: "And he said unto her, Daughter, thy faith hath made thee whole; go in peace, and be whole of thy plague" (Mark 5:34).

But God doesn't always choose to heal while we are still on Earth. Consider the apostle Paul. He suffered from a "thorn in the flesh," a condition that caused him persistent pain and difficulty (2 Corinthians 12:7). He pleaded with the Lord repeatedly to take it away, but the Lord's answer was no. Instead, the Lord offered Paul His comfort and assurance: "And he said unto me, My grace is sufficient for thee: for my strength is made perfect in weakness. Most gladly therefore will I rather glory in my infirmities, that the power of Christ may rest upon me" (2 Corinthians 12:9).

Paul's response gives us hope and resolve in the middle of our suffering.

Thrive the Way God Designed

God created our bodies to thrive on proper sleep, regular exercise, and balanced nutrition. While the Bible doesn't focus extensively on these specific health practices, it does contain several verses that highlight their value. Consider these promises about restful sleep:

Sleep

- "I will both lay me down in peace, and sleep: for thou, Lord, only makest me dwell in safety" (Psalm 4:8).
- "When thou liest down, thou shalt not be afraid: yea, thou shalt lie down, and thy sleep shall be sweet" (Proverbs 3:24).

Anxiety can disrupt our sleep in many ways, but God designed our rest to be peaceful and sweet.

Exercise

- "For bodily exercise profiteth little: but godliness is profitable unto all things, having promise of the life that now is, and of that which is to come" (1 Timothy 4:8).

While the eternal rewards of godliness far surpass the temporary benefits of physical training, that doesn't mean we should dismiss its value.

Nutrition

- "And God said, Behold, I have given you every herb bearing seed, which is upon the face of all the earth, and every tree, in the which is the fruit of a tree yielding seed; to you it shall be for meat" (Genesis 1:29).

- "Whether therefore ye eat, or drink, or whatsoever ye do, do all to the glory of God" (1 Corinthians 10:31).

These verses remind us that honoring God includes caring for the body He designed with such intention and care. Food fuels our bodies, helping us function efficiently, maintain strength, and support overall health.

Our physical bodies are an extraordinary gift to be treasured—every cell, every heartbeat, and every breath testifies to the Creator's incredible craftsmanship. They are the temples of the Holy Spirit, created with divine precision to bring honor and glory to God.

As you reflect on these truths, consider how they might apply to your journey, and what steps you can take today.

 Your Turn: Reflection Questions and Action Steps

Pause and Reflect

1. Can you identify any physical symptoms you've experienced that might be early warning signs of anxiety or depression?

2. What are the primary sources of stress in your life right now, and how are they affecting your physical health?

3. In what ways are you prioritizing sleep, nutrition, and exercise in your daily routine? What needs to change?

4. How does it impact you to know that God created you with such intricate detail and care?

5. How does understanding that you are created in the image of God influence your sense of identity and purpose?

6. In what ways does Paul's response to his "thorn in the flesh" encourage you in your struggles?

7. What steps can you take to treat your body as the temple of the Holy Spirit?

Live It Out

1. **Establish a consistent sleep routine:** Set a regular bedtime and create a peaceful wind-down routine, such as reading Scripture or meditating on God's promises, to support restful, restorative sleep.

2. **Incorporate daily physical activity:** Engage in regular exercise throughout the week to improve physical health and reduce stress. Walk, bike, or choose another heart-healthy activity most days of the week. Follow up with gentle stretching to enhance flexibility, and aim to include strength training at least twice a week.

3. **Focus on balanced nutrition:** Nourish your body with intentional, healthy choices. Plan meals that include a variety of fruits, vegetables, lean proteins, and whole grains to maintain energy and support overall wellness.

4. **Prioritize spiritual health:** Make time each day to connect with God through prayer and reflection. Begin your morning by inviting Him to lead you, and ask for strength and wisdom to care for your body.

5. **Practice Christ-centered relaxation:** Take time to be still in God's presence. Calm your body and mind with a simple method, such as breathing slowly through your nose while meditating on Psalm 46:10a: "Be still, and know that I am God." As you inhale, focus on God's peace filling you. Gently hold your breath for a count of four, then exhale slowly through your mouth for a count of six, confident you've cast your anxiety on Him and He will be faithful to carry it (1 Peter 5:7).

6. **Engage in community support:** Stay connected to a Christ-centered community that uplifts you and shares your desire to grow physically, emotionally, and spiritually.

7. **Seek professional and spiritual guidance:** Don't hesitate to reach out to healthcare or holistic professionals for physical concerns. Seek a trusted pastor or spiritual leader for encouragement, prayer, and biblical counsel.

Can I Pray for You?

Heavenly Father, Thank You for creating us in Your image. We praise You for intricately weaving our bodies together. It's incredible to know that You skillfully designed every part of us before we were even born. Thank You for giving us systems that warn us when things aren't functioning correctly. Help us to be mindful of stress that causes anxiety and be quick to bring it to You. Give us grace and wisdom to stay focused on You and to prioritize sleep, exercise, and healthy eating. Thank You for the believers who support us when we need it. Show us when we need additional physical or spiritual help, and make us aware of Your presence in every challenge. Remind us that our bodies are the temples of Your Holy Spirit. Give us grace to live with intention, honoring You through healthy and purposeful choices. In Jesus' name, Amen.

Works Cited

1   "Is Anxiety a Permanent Disability Tag." *Cedarway Therapy*, 2022, https://cedarwaytherapy.com/tag/is-anxiety-a-permanent-disability/. Accessed 24 June 2025.

2   American Psychological Association. "Stress Effects on the Body." *American Psychological Association*, 1 Nov. 2018, https://www.apa.org/topics/stress/body. Accessed 21 May 2025.

3   Mayo Clinic. "Stress Symptoms: Effects on Your Body and Behavior." *Mayo Clinic*, 10 Aug. 2023, https://www.mayoclinic.org/healthy-lifestyle/stress-management/in-depth/stress-symptoms/art-20050987. Accessed 10 June 2025.

4   Wein, Harrison. "Good Sleep for Good Health." NIH *News in Health*, National Institutes of Health, Apr. 2021, https://newsinhealth.nih.gov/2021/04/good-sleep-good-health. Accessed 21 May 2025.

5   Firth, Joseph, et al. "Food and Mood: How Do Diet and Nutrition Affect Mental Wellbeing?" BMJ, vol. 369, 29 June 2020, https://doi.org/10.1136/bmj.m2382. Accessed 21 May 2025.

6   Mayo Clinic Staff. "Exercise: 7 Benefits of Regular Physical Activity." *Mayo Clinic*, Mayo Foundation for Medical Education and Research, 26 Aug. 2023, https://www.mayoclinic.org/healthy-lifestyle/fitness/in-depth/exercise/art-20048389. Accessed 21 May 2025.

7   Food and Agriculture Organization of the United Nations. *Soil: The Foundation of Nutrition*. FAO, 2022, https://openknowledge.fao.org/server/api/core/bitstreams/9d22c9cf-4a75-4d34-b42d-177d14eaf1ae/content. Accessed 28 Aug. 2025.

2

God's Blueprint for Physical Health

My Life Lesson

Tremors racked my body as I lay in bed after my second suicide attempt, completely drained both physically and emotionally. Prolonged, chronic depression had given way to hopeless dread. My impulsive decision unleashed a storm, affecting me at every level.

Soon after, my thoughts turned psychotic, marked by intense paranoia, disorganized thinking, and delusions. I couldn't shake the feeling that I was being watched. Whenever I left our house, I believed Steve had people tracking my every move: where I went, what I purchased, and with whom I interacted. Following conversations became nearly impossible, and my thoughts raced in endless loops. I felt bound by the invisible chains of fear and confusion—unable to break free.

When Food Became the Enemy

Anxiety, depression, and psychosis took a toll on my physical health. Anxiety robbed me of my appetite, and psychosis only deepened the struggle. Paranoia tightened its grip. I became overwhelmed with the thought that Steve was poisoning my food and water.

Fear consumed me. I tried to control every aspect of our meals, from grocery shopping to food preparation, desperate to ensure their safety. There was only one problem: getting ready was already draining, so the simplest tasks seemed impossible. Creating a grocery list? Too much work. At the store, my thoughts scattered. I wandered the aisles aimlessly, struggling to find what I needed. Finally, my husband would gather the items while I stood by the cart, unable to make the smallest decisions.

As he placed things in the cart, I instinctively reorganized them. I was determined to keep everything separate, sure that even the slightest touch would cause contamination. With every addition, the buggy filled, and my concern increased. By the time we reached the checkout counter, I felt defeated. The food, now tainted in my mind, seemed beyond salvaging. Why should I take it home when I was certain it would poison me? In my psychotic state, I believed Steve was immune to the food's effects, yet intent on getting me to eat it, forcing me to suffer the consequences. Even after leaving the store, the anxiety followed me home.

Fear in the Familiar Places

As soon as we walked through the door, a new suspicion took hold—the refrigerator had been tampered with. As I unpacked the food, the thought lingered. What if the system regulating the temperature had failed? There could only be one conclusion: everything inside would spoil, making me sick. As I struggled with a lack of appetite, focusing on the possibility only made it harder to eat.

Mornings were the hardest. Ongoing fatigue made it difficult to get out of bed, and the thought of breakfast turned my stomach. Knowing I needed to gain weight, Steve encouraged me to eat two eggs and buttered toast instead of my usual quarter cup of oatmeal. Sitting alone at the dining room table, I would let my breakfast get cold long before I managed to eat half of it. Nothing tasted right, and the smells were enough to make me gag. Lunch and dinner weren't much better.

I let distorted thinking and altered senses shape my reality, allowing them to guide my decisions. Convinced that the refrigerator had caused the food to spoil, I knew I had to take action.

Over the next few days, while my husband was occupied with meetings and calls, I took matters into my own hands: I took apart the back of the refrigerator, removed the panels, scrubbed the coils, and sterilized everything in a desperate attempt to fix it. Yet doubt lingered, keeping me trapped in fear.

A New Battle: The Water Dilemma

As if food weren't enough of a concern, water presented another battle. Choosing a brand that didn't taste strange became an exhausting challenge. We walked down the store aisle as I analyzed every option: spring, mineral, artesian, purified. *Should I go for pH-neutral water? Or one with electrolytes?* The number of options overwhelmed me. After fifteen minutes, I still hadn't added a single bottle to the cart. Fear of making the wrong choice paralyzed me. Tired of waiting, my husband gave me a time limit, forcing me to make a decision.

Even after we returned home, my apprehension followed. When Steve stored the bottled water in the garage, my fears escalated. My online searches fed my growing suspicion, fueling intrusive thoughts. I imagined he had rigged a complex system using the garage door mechanism and other materials to change the water's composition, making it unsafe to drink. The longer the bottles sat in the garage, the more contaminated they became—or so I believed. I avoided them whenever possible, eventually coming up with a plan to keep from drinking them altogether.

Whenever I ran an errand, I would stop at the nearest gas station, purchase the largest bottle of water available, and finish it before returning home. Despite my fears, I kept them to myself, afraid of backlash—feeling like a disobedient child failing to meet expectations. But my chronic suspicion and irrational behavior led to countless arguments, each one adding to the strain on our relationship.

From Breakdown to Breakthrough

For nine long months, I was trapped in paranoia, fear, and physical decline. But everything changed on September 1, 2023, when I experienced the Lord's miraculous healing. Yet the effects of two and a half years of stress on my body didn't disappear overnight. Knowing I needed to establish a baseline, I had bloodwork drawn. The results revealed a harsh truth. I was dealing with several physical issues:

- Pre-diabetes
- High cholesterol
- Non-alcoholic fatty liver
- Vitamin D3 and vitamin B12 deficiencies
- Dehydration
- Thyroid issues
- Hormonal imbalance

Eager to act on my holistic doctor's advice, I started a conservative supplement regimen. When I repeated the bloodwork roughly five months later, the results had improved significantly. Although everything wasn't back to normal, things were moving in the right direction:

- One of the two liver enzymes was in the normal range (formerly high risk)
- Vitamin D3 and vitamin B12 were now within the normal range
- Hormones were regulated

Today, as I care for the body God has entrusted to me, through nourishing food, exercise, rest, and supplements, I feel my best and have renewed strength.

What step is the Lord inviting you to take? Whether it's reaching out for support, making a change in your routine, or simply choosing to rest, healing often begins with one obedient step at a time.

The Science Behind It

Science confirms what Scripture and experience already suggest: our physical and mental health are connected by God's design.

What we eat matters. Nutrition plays a vital role in supporting how our bodies function every day. The food we choose affects everything: from how we process macronutrients (carbohydrates, fats, and proteins) and absorb micronutrients (vitamins and minerals) to how we manage blood sugar and maintain gut health. When we prioritize a balanced diet rich in whole, nourishing foods, we supply our bodies with what they need, not just for physical health but for mental clarity and emotional stability.

Consider two scenarios. Salmon, walnuts, avocados, and spinach—foods rich in omega-3 fatty acids—have been shown to reduce symptoms of anxiety and depression. These healthy fats help protect and support our brain cells.[1] On the other hand, diets high in processed foods and sugars can increase inflammation and disrupt blood sugar levels, resulting in mood swings.[2]

Nutritional Deficiencies That Affect the Brain

God created our bodies to thrive when we give them the right building blocks. Whole foods supply the vitamins and nutrients our brains need for optimal function and over-all health. When we're deficient in certain nutrients, it can lead to chemical changes in the brain, making us more vulnerable to mental health struggles.[3] Here are a few that play a significant role:

- **Vitamin D**: Often called the "sunshine vitamin," low levels of vitamin D have been linked to depression and other mood disorders.

- **B vitamins**: B6, B9 (folate), and B12 are essential for healthy brain function. Deficiencies can interfere with the production of mood-regulating neurotransmitters.

- **Magnesium**: This mineral supports relaxation and emotional balance. Low levels can intensify symptoms of anxiety and depression.

- **Omega-3 fatty acids**: These healthy fats are vital for brain health. Inadequate intake may contribute to emotional instability and persistent low mood.[4]

Hormonal Imbalances and Mental Health

Our bodies also rely on a delicate hormonal balance: God's intricate communication system within us. Hormones influence everything from metabolism and sleep to stress levels and mood. When there's an imbalance, either too much or too little of a hormone, things can feel off physically and emotionally.[5] Some common imbalances include:

- **Cortisol**: Known as the "stress hormone," high levels of cortisol can leave us feeling on edge and mentally exhausted over time.[6]

- **Thyroid hormones**: Too much or too little thyroid hormone can affect energy, concentration, and mood.[7]
- **Estrogen and progesterone**: These female hormones fluctuate with menstrual cycles and life stages, often influencing mood and anxiety levels.[8]
- **Testosterone**: Though often associated with men, this hormone also affects mood regulation in women.[9]

When multiple imbalances occur, like low levels of vitamin B alongside elevated cortisol, the chances of facing more intense mental health struggles increase. That's why it's so important to pray about our physical health, make wise choices concerning nutrition and lifestyle, and seek medical support when needed.

Why Gut Health Matters—And What to Do About It

Our Creator didn't just design our bodies with care; He created remarkable systems of communication between the different parts. One of the most fascinating is the link between the gut and brain. Known as the gut-brain axis, this connection involves:

- **The nervous system:** particularly the vagus nerve, which carries signals between the gut and brain
- **The immune system:** inflammation in the gut can influence mood and cognitive function
- **The hormonal system:** certain hormones produced in the gut impact brain activity
- **The microbiota:** trillions of gut bacteria that help create neurotransmitters like serotonin[10]

As Dr. Mike Hoaglin, the San Francisco-based medical director of the telehealth company DrHouse, explains: "There's one neurotransmitter, in particular, that's made in high supply in the gut: serotonin, often referred to as the 'feel good' hormone. And while you might think that serotonin would be made in the brain—and some of it is—a whopping 95% of our body's serotonin is made in our guts."[11]

When our gut is in good health, the brain responds by producing mood-enhancing chemicals such as serotonin, dopamine, and oxytocin.[12] Together, this powerful combination supports both our physical and emotional well-being.

Earlier, we looked at how nutrition impacts the body as a whole. Here, let's focus more specifically on what you can do to support your gut:

- **Eat whole, nutrient-rich foods:** Choose a variety of fruits, vegetables, lean proteins, and whole grains. These supply fiber that feeds beneficial gut bacteria.

- **Include probiotic and prebiotic foods:** Fermented foods, such as yogurt, kefir, and sauerkraut, provide healthy bacteria, while foods like garlic, onions, and bananas support their growth.

- **Stay hydrated:** Water supports digestion and nutrient absorption.

- **Limit processed and high-sugar foods:** They can disrupt the balance of gut bacteria and increase inflammation.

- **Manage stress and move your body:** Stress can directly impact digestion, while regular physical activity promotes healthy gut function.[13]

Even small, intentional changes in these areas can make a significant difference. Caring for gut health means caring for our mind and emotions, too. However, it's also important to remember that gut health is just one piece of the bigger picture. Anxiety and depression often have complex roots, shaped by a mix of nutrient and hormone imbalances, unresolved childhood trauma, unhelpful thought patterns, and spiritual wounds.

That's why one of the wisest and simplest next steps is getting lab work done. Blood tests can reveal deficiencies or imbalances that might be affecting our physical or mental health.

Understanding what's going on inside our bodies helps us move forward with clarity and a plan to be good stewards of the health God has entrusted to us.

Help and Hope from God's Word

Though I didn't realize it at the time, the anxiety, fatigue, and intrusive thoughts weren't just emotional or physical; they revealed a deeper spiritual battle. The enemy had subtly twisted my view of God's good gifts, using fear to plant seeds of doubt.

My struggle with food and water had never been about nutrition—it was about trust. The very things intended to strengthen my body became sources of anxiety, because I was wrestling for control.

Let's journey back to the Garden of Eden. It began with the enemy's lie, and his tactics haven't changed. With a single question, the serpent cast doubt in Eve's mind: "Yea, hath God said, Ye shall not eat of every tree of the garden?" (Genesis 3:1b).

That question made Eve pause and consider. Was God holding something back? Sensing her hesitation, Satan took advantage of the moment, offering a tempting promise: Eat the fruit, and you'll be like God, knowing both good and evil.

Eve had no idea how high the stakes were. Notice what she did next: she relied on what she could see and touch. Scripture tells us: "And when the woman saw that the tree was good for food, and that it was pleasant to the eyes, and a tree to be desired to make one wise, she took of the fruit thereof, and did eat, and gave also unto her husband with her; and he did eat" (Genesis 3:6).

We all know the consequences of Adam and Eve's actions. Sin entered the world, and the couple was sent from the garden, no longer able to eat from the tree of life.

The Choices We Make

Like Eve, I've made decisions based on my senses, maybe you have too. Yet our senses, though given by God, aren't always reliable. During psychosis, the unappetizing smell of food led me to believe it was harmful rather than nourishing. On the other hand, just because food smells delicious and looks appetizing doesn't mean it's the best choice to nourish our bodies.

Satan has long used food as a tool to distract and deceive, just as he did in the beginning. But God created food to nourish our bodies and to strengthen us for the work He's called us to do. Have you noticed how Satan subtly shifts our focus from the outcome—fulfilling God's work—to the resource that fuels it: the food itself?

When we start viewing food as the goal rather than a means to achieve our purpose, we often fall into unhealthy patterns, whether it's avoiding food altogether, like I did, or indulging in sugary, salty, and processed foods. Whether we overeat or undereat, it makes no difference to the enemy. The result is the same: our focus shifts from God's plan to our desires.

I let food rule my life, avoiding it out of fear, focusing on the food rather than the One who gave it to me. Do you see the enemy's trap? We create a false god that can never bring true satisfaction.

The Example to Follow

So, how do we resist these traps? Jesus' temptation in the wilderness gives us an excellent example of how to overcome trials involving food: "Then was Jesus led up of the Spirit into the wilderness to be tempted of the devil. And when he had fasted forty days and forty nights, he was afterward an hungred. And when the tempter came to him, he said, If thou be the Son of God, command that these stones be made bread" (Matthew 4:1–3).

Notice when the devil approached Jesus: it was at His most vulnerable, after fasting for an extended period. His body was undoubtedly weak, and Scripture emphasizes that He was hungry. The enemy wasted no time and began by attacking Jesus' identity. If He truly was the Son of God, as He claimed, surely He could turn stones into bread.

Yet Jesus remained unshaken. He didn't mount a defense or argue, He simply responded: "But he answered and said, It is written, Man shall not live by bread alone, but by every word that proceedeth out of the mouth of God" (Matthew 4:4).

It was not the right time for Jesus to eat. By quoting Deuteronomy 8:3, He emphasized that the source of bread matters more than the bread itself. His strength came from doing the will of the Father, and the same is true for you and me.

Much like the enemy tempted Jesus when He was physically weak, I see now how fear and confusion clouded my judgment during psychosis, making food seem dangerous rather than sustaining. But while Jesus clung to God's truth rather than taking the bait Satan offered, I had to let go of my fear and reestablish trust in His provision instead of my distorted perceptions.

The Way to Victory

So, how do we apply these principles when we face temptations with food?

- **Recognize** when you are most vulnerable: such as when you're tired, stressed, lonely, or already discouraged.
- **Remember**, your God-given purpose is more important than focusing on the food.

- **Rely** on God's Word and speak His truth over your situation.

When we acknowledge our weaknesses, stay focused on our divine purpose, and combat temptation with God's truth, we can walk in victory. Jesus meets our deepest longings and provides for our physical needs as well: "And Jesus said unto them, I am the bread of life: he that cometh to me shall never hunger; and he that believeth on me shall never thirst" (John 6:35).

Today, as I fill my mind with God's truth and submit to His guidance, I no longer view food with fear but as a gift from a good and trustworthy Heavenly Father. I can enjoy it, confident in His provision and care.

 ## Your Turn: Reflection Questions and Action Steps

Pause and Reflect

1. Have physical and mental health challenges impacted your daily life and relationships? If so, what strategies are helping you navigate these difficulties?

2. How does your current diet impact your overall well-being, and what steps can you take to incorporate more whole foods and essential nutrients?

3. In what ways might vitamin deficiencies or hormone imbalances be affecting your mental health, and how can you address these issues through nutrition and lifestyle changes?

4. Considering the gut-brain connection, what changes can you make to improve your gut health, and how might these changes influence your mental and emotional state?

5. In what ways might Satan be subtly distracting you from your God-given purpose, even through something as ordinary as your food choices?

6. In what ways do you rely on your senses to make decisions, and how can you ensure that your choices align more closely with God's will rather than your immediate desires?

7. Reflecting on Jesus' response to temptation in the wilderness, how can you use Scripture and spiritual disciplines to strengthen your resolve against temptations in your life?

Live It Out

1. **Establish a baseline for health:** Have comprehensive blood work done to identify underlying health issues, such as vitamin deficiencies, hormone imbalances, or other concerns. This will provide a clear picture of your physical health and guide necessary adjustments.

2. **Incorporate whole foods:** Include more fruits, vegetables, lean proteins, whole grains, and healthy fats. These provide essential nutrients for optimal brain and body function.

3. **Monitor vitamin levels:** Regularly check your vitamin levels, particularly vitamin D, B vitamins, and magnesium. Consider supplements if needed

and make dietary adjustments to ensure you're getting sufficient amounts of these crucial nutrients.

4. **Support gut health:** Maintain a healthy gut by consuming foods rich in probiotics and prebiotics, such as yogurt, kefir, sauerkraut, kimchi, and fibrous vegetables. A healthy gut benefits your mood and overall well-being.

5. **Identify vulnerabilities:** Take note of when you are most susceptible to temptation, whether it's when you're hungry, stressed, or tired. Recognizing these moments can help you prepare and equip yourself to resist temptation more effectively.

6. **Align with God's purpose**: Regularly remind yourself of your God-given purpose and how your choices align with it. Focus on the work you are called to do rather than distractions or temptations.

7. **Use Scripture as a defense:** Just as Jesus used Scripture to resist temptation, memorize and meditate on Bible verses that strengthen your resolve and provide guidance during times of temptation.

Can I Pray for You?

Heavenly Father, We come before You with grateful hearts, in awe of the way You've knit our bodies together. Thank You for the gift of nutrition and the wisdom to understand how what we eat affects both our physical and mental well-being. Help us make mindful choices—

nourishing our bodies with the good things You have provided, and turning away from the habits that can lead to anxiety, depression, and other health issues. Give us the discipline to include wholesome, balanced meals that supply the nutrients our bodies and brains need. We lift our vitamin and hormone levels to You, knowing how deficiencies can affect our emotions and clarity of mind. Equip us with wisdom to recognize when we need help, whether through dietary changes, supplements, or medical care. Father, we also recognize the significant connection between our gut and our mental health. Strengthen us to make choices that support healing from the inside out. Most of all, help us look to You as the Bread of Life. Teach us to love You more than the gift of food, to cling to Your truth when temptation comes, and to find our ultimate satisfaction in You. In Jesus' name, Amen.

Works Cited

1. Mischoulon, David. "Omega-3 Fatty Acids for Mood Disorders." *Harvard Health Blog*, 3 Aug. 2018, https://www.health.harvard.edu/blog/omega-3-fatty-acids-for-mood-disorders-2018080314414. Accessed 28 May 2025.

2. Salamon, Maureen. "Ultraprocessed Foods May Raise Depression Risks." *Harvard Health*, 1 Jan. 2024, https://www.health.harvard.edu/mind-and-mood/ultraprocessed-foods-may-raise-depression-risks. Accessed 28 May 2025.

3. "9 Vitamin and Nutritional Deficiencies That May Cause Depression" *Psych Central*, 25 Aug. 2021, https://psychcentral.com/blog/nutritional-deficiencies-that-may-cause-depression. Accessed 28 May 2025.

4. "9 Vitamin and Nutritional Deficiencies That May Cause Depression" *Psych Central*, 25 Aug. 2021, https://psychcentral.com/blog/nutritional-deficiencies-that-may-cause-depression. Accessed 28 May 2025.

5. "Hormones: The Key to Unlocking Optimal Health." *Modern Endocrine*, 15 Nov. 2024, https://www.modern-endocrine.com/hormones-the-key-to-unlocking-optimal-health/. Accessed 28 May 2025.

6. NeuroLaunch Editorial Team. "Cortisol and Anxiety: The Intricate Relationship and Stress-Hormone Connection." *NeuroLaunch.com*, 18 Aug. 2024, https://neurolaunch.com/cortisol-and-anxiety/. Accessed 28 May 2025.

7. WebMD Editorial Contributors. "Depression, the Thyroid, and Hormones." *WebMD*, https://www.webmd.com/depression/depression-the-thyroid-and-hormones. Accessed 28 May 2025.

8. "The Effects of Estrogen on Women's Emotions and Mood." *WebMD*, 2022, https://www.webmd.com/women/estrogen-and-womens-emotions. Accessed 28 May 2025.

9. "The Impact of Testosterone on Mood: Understanding the Hormone's Role." *Medshun*, 21 Jan. 2024, https://medshun.com/article/how-does-testosterone-affect-mood. Accessed 28 May 2025.

10. Sherrell, Zia. "What Is the Gut-Brain Connection." *Medical News Today*, Healthline Media, 8 Sept. 2023, https://www.medicalnewstoday.com/articles/gut-brain-connection. Accessed 28 May 2025.

11. Haddad-Garcia, Maria Laura. "How Poor Gut Health Can Increase Anxiety and Depression Risk & What to Eat to Help." *EatingWell*, Dotdash Meredith, https://www.eatingwell.com/article/8001367/poor-gut-health-increases-anxiety-depression-risk-what-to-eat/. Accessed 30 May 2025.

12 Haddad-Garcia, Maria Laura. "How Poor Gut Health Can Increase Anxiety and Depression Risk & What to Eat to Help." *EatingWell*, Dotdash Meredith, https://www.eatingwell.com/article/8001367/poor-gut-health-increases-anxiety-depression-risk-what-to-eat/. Accessed 30 May 2025.

13 Mayo Clinic Staff. "The Microbiome and Its Influence on Healthy Aging." *Mayo Clinic Press*, Mayo Foundation for Medical Education and Research, 7 Sept. 2023, https://mcpress.mayoclinic.org/healthygut/the-microbiome-and-its-influence-on-healthy-aging. Accessed 26 August 2025.

Part 2:
Your Soul—Mind, Heart, and Will

3

What Am I Thinking and How Does It Affect Me?

My Life Lesson

It may sound unusual, but it's important to question our thoughts. Where do they come from? Are they rooted in truth? What emotions do they stir? And how do these emotions, in turn, shape our thoughts?

What we focus on shapes our emotions, and those emotions drive our thoughts and actions. It becomes a cycle that can either help or harm. Anxiety and depression often distort both our thoughts and feelings, pulling them in a negative direction. That's why it's vital to have people in our lives who speak words of truth, especially when our inner narrative becomes distorted.

Without intentionally monitoring our thoughts and emotions—and without the perspective of someone we trust—it's easy to embrace lies that spiral out of control. I found myself trapped there, unable to escape.

The First Episode

It was early fall 2006. A friend and I were driving home from a trip to a beautiful waterfall when the accident occurred. The sound of metal scraping against metal was followed by a jarring impact as our vehicles collided. It all happened so quickly. As my SUV rolled to a stop, I sat behind the wheel, completely stunned.

At first, I was shaken, but I seemed physically fine. Yet, within days, waves of panic began to rise. The darkness crept in slowly, along with a feeling I had never experienced before. I knew I needed help.

Over the next several months, I visited my primary care doctor, spoke with a Christian counselor, and practiced strategies to stay calm and focused, including deep breathing, writing out and memorizing Scripture, and listening to worship music.

I welcomed the hard work of journaling and found joy in the outlet it provided. Within nine months, the fog gradually lifted. I re-engaged with life, even though the cause of my anxiety remained a mystery.

But as my routine returned to normal, I slowly drifted from the habits that had helped me. I slipped into autopilot. I hadn't planned what to do if anxiety returned—maybe because, deep down, I didn't want to believe it ever would.

When the Past Returns

More than fifteen years had passed since that episode, so I was alarmed when familiar symptoms resurfaced in 2021. It began with racing thoughts, creeping dread, and an overwhelming sense of fear.

I remember the night I was unable to sleep. Standing at the kitchen counter the next day, my fingers tapping a nervous rhythm on the cool surface, I wrestled to form the words to tell my husband what I already knew: the anxiety was back. *How could this be happening again?*

I had naïvely assumed I was no longer vulnerable. A confusing mix of pride and shame flooded my mind. I didn't want to admit I had surrendered to fear, yet the sensations in my body and my spiraling thoughts made it undeniable.

The moment felt surreal. I struggled to give voice to my thoughts, afraid that once spoken, the words would somehow define me. I managed to get them out. I described the restlessness, the panic, the growing certainty that something was wrong. Steve was incredibly supportive and encouraging, helping me seek professional care.

Together, we returned to the tools that had helped before. I met with a Christian counselor, took medication for stabilization, revisited Bible verses on anxiety, practiced deep breathing, and returned to journaling. I reminded myself that healing had taken nine months the first time and began counting the days. But this time, relief didn't come. As weeks turned into months, discouragement set in. Hope slowly slipped away.

Lies I Believed

In my desperation, I chased every possible explanation: anything to stop what I was feeling. The lack of control was disorienting. Over a two-and-a-half-year span, one subtle lie snowballed into many. I felt powerless to resist:

- *I am not worthy to teach or facilitate the book study.* (initial lie)
- *I need to step back from all ministry.*
- *I can't tell my friends I'm struggling because they will think poorly of me.*
- *No one can help me.*
- *I can't go on like this.*
- *I must not be a Christian.*

Looking back, I see what had changed between my first and second encounters with anxiety. The first time, I fought hard, reaching out for help, leaning on God's truth, and refusing to give up. But this time, physically exhausted and mentally drained, I stopped fighting. Instead of remembering I had overcome this before, I gave in to the fear.

Because I didn't understand the root cause, my thinking went like this: *I must have done something wrong, and God is punishing me, otherwise, I wouldn't feel this way.* I listened to the lie and stopped challenging my thoughts. Little by little, I began to believe the lie that no one, not even God, could help me.

The Depths of Darkness

After I had battled anxiety and depression for almost two years—surviving two suicide attempts—those closest to me could tell something was seriously wrong. At first, my symptoms were difficult to define. But as they dragged on, troubling signs emerged: paranoia, disorganized thinking, emotional withdrawal, chronic insomnia, and a sharp decline in even basic self-care.[1] It was psychosis.

Steve noticed a distinct change in my behavior one evening when he came home from a mandatory business trip. Our daughter and son-in-law had graciously agreed to come and stay with me while he was away. When he got back, I was tense and withdrawn, and I refused to share my thoughts with him. For the first few days after his return, I stayed silent, unable—or unwilling—to voice the thoughts raging in my mind. His constant questioning exasperated me, and finally, I opened up.

I revealed that I believed he and our family were spying on me through hidden cameras and doing countless things to harm me. I told him I deserved it for the emotional distress I had caused them. Until then, he had suspected something was deeply wrong, but the depth and direction of my thoughts came as a complete shock.

His response was one of disbelief. Hurt and anger were evident in his words. The conflict that followed shut me down.

Irrational Beliefs and Everyday Life

Following the volatile exchange, I refused to trust anyone but myself. I kept my feelings to myself, all the while think-ing the worst. Even after I confessed some of my thoughts to Steve, I didn't share every irrational belief I had. Although some remained locked away, my actions began to expose the layers of the conspiracy theory I had embraced.

I was afraid to shower, convinced Steve had set the water to scalding, so I began washing with isopropyl rubbing alcohol instead. Each evening, I would wipe down the bedding with Clorox wipes to sanitize everything.

I went weeks without brushing my teeth because I was sure the toothpaste contained toxins. Afraid some of my prescription medication had been tampered with, I would often pretend to take the pills, only to wrap them up in a napkin and throw them away later. I avoided our cats and dog, believing they had microbes that could make me sick. The list of irrational thoughts was endless.

Steve's Love and My Resistance

Throughout my battle, Steve continued to speak truth into my life, confronting the lies I believed and reminding me what was real. He kept trying to break through, even when my words and actions made little sense to him. He never gave up. Even when I pushed him away, he reminded me the battle wasn't my fault—he still loved me and longed to see me restored.

I can only imagine the helplessness he felt, watching me slip further away. However, the longer the anxiety and depression dragged on, the more I resisted my husband's counsel. Every piece of advice, encouragement, and information he shared was filtered through my growing suspicion. Eventually, I stopped listening to him altogether.

The more I relied on my understanding, the more entangled I became in the lies that replayed in my mind. All my relationships were strained, especially those with my husband and family. I forfeited the peace that comes from trusting the Lord, turning from the very path that could have led me out of psychosis and away from the enemy's trap.

That peace was offered in God's Word: "Trust in the Lord with all thine heart; and lean not unto thine own understanding. In all thy ways acknowledge him, and he shall direct thy paths" (Proverbs 3:5–6).

The Battle for the Mind

Both times I faced anxiety and depression, I assumed the struggle was purely spiritual. But over time, I began to see the truth. My body and mind were just as much a part of the battle. The longer I remained in the valley, the stronger the temptation became to let my thoughts and emotions run unchecked—until psychosis stripped me of the ability to receive counsel from my husband and others who cared for me.

Knowing what's at stake, we must learn to monitor our thoughts and invite those we trust to speak truth into our lives. It's a principle worth holding onto: taking our thoughts captive, realigning them with God's truth, and listening to those who speak words of hope when we can't hear them for ourselves.

The Science Behind It

There's no doubt: we are fearfully and wonderfully made by the God of the universe (Psalm 139:14). He created our bodies with great intentionality, including the intricate design of our brains. While I'm not a cognitive scientist, I've come to see the value of understanding how the brain works, especially in anxiety and depression.

When Anxiety Takes Over

So, what happens in our brains when we experience anxiety? God designed our brains to respond quickly to danger, whether the threat is real or perceived. This built-in survival system is often called the "fight-or-flight" response, and it involves three key parts:

- **Amygdala:** scans for threats and sounds the alarm
- **Hypothalamus:** signals the body to activate the sympathetic nervous system, raising heart rate, dilating pupils, relaxing airways, slowing digestion, and releasing glucose and stress hormones
- **Adrenal glands:** release adrenaline and cortisol, providing a burst of energy and increased alertness[2]

How Depression Affects the Brain

While this response is helpful in actual emergencies, when the system is overactive or misfiring, as is common in anxiety, it can leave us feeling panicked and exhausted.[3]

Similarly, depression also affects our brains. It doesn't just alter how we feel; it also impacts how our brain is wired. Research shows it can lead to several changes in both the structure and function of the brain, including:

- **Reduction in gray matter:** especially in the prefrontal cortex, hippocampus, and thalamus, areas that help regulate thinking, memory, and emotions[4]
- **Shrinkage of the hippocampus:** critical for learning and memory, it can shrink in response to prolonged stress, often linked to elevated cortisol levels[5]
- **An overactive amygdala:** becomes hyper-alert, often resulting in strong emotional reactions and a negative view of circumstances[6]

These changes don't just stay hidden inside the brain; they show up in everyday life:

- **Memory problems:** difficulty focusing or recalling information[7]
- **A negative lens:** a tendency to remember and dwell on negative experiences more than positive ones[8]
- **Low motivation:** a lack of drive or energy, making it harder to complete daily tasks[9]

The Trap of Distorted Thinking

In my own life, anxiety and depression were closely intertwined. By the time I recognized the physical symptoms of anxiety (racing heart, shallow breathing, restlessness), my thoughts were already spiraling into depression. My thinking was riddled with cognitive distortions—mental traps that kept me stuck in fear and hopelessness. Looking back, I can now identify several specific distortions that shaped my thinking.

- **All-or-nothing thinking:** It is the tendency to see things in black-and-white terms, with no middle ground. For example, because I struggled with anxiety, I believed I was unworthy to serve in ministry and stepped back from everything.
- **Mental filtering:** This occurs when a person focuses only on the negative aspects of a situation while ignoring the positive. For example, during psychosis, I believed I had always been a bad wife and mother, even though my family told me otherwise.
- **Catastrophizing:** This is the tendency to imagine the worst-case scenario. For example, at one point, I was sure I had a rare disease and was dying.
- **Emotional reasoning:** It is the belief that your feelings reflect reality. For instance, I felt like a fail-

ure, which led me to believe I was one.

- **Control fallacies:** These occur when someone feels either helpless and controlled by others or compelled to control everything. For instance, I thought I had to disinfect everything to avoid dying from germ exposure.
- **"Should" statements:** These involve using "should" to criticize yourself or others, leading to guilt or frustration. For example, I believed I should be perfect to serve in ministry and felt intense guilt when I wasn't.[10]

Although my journey included the rare experience of psychosis, disordered thinking is something many of us face, often in more subtle, everyday ways. Unhealthy thought patterns are surprisingly common, even if we don't recognize them at the time. Negative self-talk, in particular, is a common thread woven through seasons of anxiety and depression. If left unchecked, these thought patterns can begin to take root and shape our view of ourselves, others, and even God.

Surrendering Every Thought

Can you relate to any of these unhealthy thinking patterns? Scripture invites us to view health holistically, recognizing that our physical, emotional, and spiritual well-being are deeply connected. That's why our thought life matters. It's worth asking: *Is my thinking grounded in truth?*

Are there negative thought patterns we need to identify, surrender, and reshape in a way that honors God? When our thoughts align with His truth, we begin to experience greater wholeness in every part of our lives.

Help and Hope from God's Word

God's Word lays out a detailed blueprint for our thought life, especially when we're overwhelmed by anxiety or fear. Paul paints a beautiful picture of what it looks like to surrender our thoughts to God and experience His peace:

> Be careful for nothing; but in every thing by prayer and supplication with thanksgiving let your requests be made known unto God. And the peace of God, which passeth all understanding, shall keep your hearts and minds through Christ Jesus. Finally, brethren, whatsoever things are true, whatsoever things are honest, whatsoever things are just, whatsoever things are pure, whatsoever things are lovely, whatsoever things are of good report; if there be any virtue, and if there be any praise, think on these things.
>
> —Philippians 4:6–8

Starting with Surrender

When we find ourselves consumed by worry, Jesus invites us to come to Him in prayer and lay our concerns at His feet. What a thought. The King of the Universe welcomes us to talk with Him any time we're troubled. When we surrender our worries to Him, something incredible happens. We experience a peace beyond understanding.

That supernatural peace is paired with a practical next step: guarding our minds. Are we focusing on what's true and right? This passage offers us a kind of litmus test for our thoughts—a way to evaluate whether they align with God's truth. Thoughts that don't pass the test can be discarded; those that do can remain.

But it doesn't stop there. We're also called to take purposeful steps that keep us actively engaged in the spiritual battle we face. Consider the timeless counsel and encouragement Paul shared with the Corinthians:

For though we walk in the flesh, we do not war after the flesh: (For the weapons of our warfare are not carnal, but mighty through God to the pulling down of strong holds;) Casting down imaginations, and every high thing that exalteth itself against the knowledge of God, and bringing into captivity every thought to the obedience of Christ;

—2 Corinthians 10:3–5

Tearing Down Strongholds

Notice what Paul is saying here: our human strategies alone cannot win spiritual battles. To tear down and overcome strongholds, we must rely on the Holy Spirit and spiritual weapons. In this context, a stronghold is a deeply ingrained pattern of thinking that binds us, keeping us from embracing God's truth and will. It may sound intimidating, but we're not left defenseless. God has equipped us with everything we need to overcome these mental strongholds. Consider each resource carefully:

- **Prayer:** honest communication with God, seeking His will, wisdom, and direction
- **Scripture:** using God's Word to counteract false teachings and negative thoughts
- **Faith:** trusting God's power and promises to overcome challenges

- **Righteousness:** living according to God's principles to stand firm against spiritual attacks
- **Spiritual discernment:** recognizing and rejecting deceptive thoughts and influences

God has given us powerful weapons—tools we can use daily as we fight these mental and spiritual battles. It isn't easy, even in the absence of anxiety and depression. That's why it's called a battle. In the middle of anxiety and depression, letting go of negative thinking patterns that trap you in a repetitive, ruminating cycle can feel impossible. I remember being trapped in that cycle of defeat. But there is hope.

Renewing Our Mind

Along with clear examples of what to focus on and an arsenal of spiritual weapons to fight and overcome the stronghold of negative thinking, God also provides us with further guidance to help renew our minds: "And be not conformed to this world: but be ye transformed by the renewing of your mind, that ye may prove what is that good, and acceptable, and perfect, will of God" (Romans 12:2).

This verse reminds us not to pattern our thoughts and behaviors after the world's way of thinking, a mindset shaped by sin, materialism, and self-centeredness. During my struggle with anxiety and depression, my focus shifted away from my Savior and onto myself. The more I tried to stay in control, the harder it became to pray.

When we surrender our grip on control and align our thoughts with God's truth, He begins to transform us from the inside out, renewing our minds and strengthening us to resist the world's influence. We discover that His purpose for our lives is good, acceptable, and deeply fulfilling.

Put Off, Put On: Living in Your New Identity

Several more helpful verses are found in the book of Ephesians: "That ye put off concerning the former conversation the old man, which is corrupt according to the deceitful lusts; And be renewed in the spirit of your mind; And that ye put on the new man, which after God is created in righteousness and true holiness" (Ephesians 4:22–24).

These verses challenge us not only to renew our minds but also to "put off" the old and "put on" the new. This imagery is powerful. When we accept Christ as our Savior, we become "new creatures" (2 Corinthians 5:17). Yet we continue to live in human bodies wrestling with weakness and sin (Romans 7:19). We're called to take off the behaviors of the old life—like dirty clothes—and to put on thoughts and actions that reflect our identity in Christ.

These new clothes are stunning. They reflect God's righteousness and holiness. What a beautiful image of the transformation only He can bring. I vividly remember how, during the three weeks between *The Day of Truth* and my healing, God reminded me I was His child. Remaining clothed in the rags of anxiety and depression was not who I was. Through loving accountability and constant reminders of God's grace, it was as if He gently removed the filthy rags, one layer at a time. In their place, God offered fresh, clean garments. I couldn't refuse His offer.

Because of our relationship with our Heavenly Father, He has given us everything we need to be overcomers in our thought lives. Embrace your identity in Christ.

Freedom Found in Truth

Yes, we are engaged in a fierce spiritual battle. To stand firm, we must cry out to the Lord for help, identifying flawed thought patterns and replacing them with truth. When we do, God offers us an incredible promise: "And ye shall know the truth, and the truth shall make you free" (John 8:32).

As truth takes root, the lies lose their grip, and we begin to walk in freedom. The God who equips us with truth also walks beside us, empowering us to replace negative, critical thoughts with ones filled with hope and gratitude. He is faithful to renew our minds and restore our peace.

Your Turn: Reflection Questions and Action Steps

Pause and Reflect

1. Reflect on how anxiety and depression have impacted your thoughts and behaviors.

2. Can you identify any cognitive distortions or strongholds (e.g., all-or-nothing thinking, mental filtering, catastrophizing, "should" statements) in your thinking? Write down a recent example.

3. In moments of anxiety or depression, have you been able to pray and lay your concerns before the Lord? Reflect on what you experienced.

4. Take a moment to examine your current thoughts. Hold them up against the list in Philippians 4:8. Do they reflect the qualities mentioned there?

5. Identify any thoughts that don't align with those qualities. How can you use the spiritual weapons

of prayer, Scripture, faith, righteousness, and discernment to tear down these strongholds?

6. Consider Romans 12:2 and Ephesians 4:22–24. What practical steps can you take to renew your mind and align your thoughts with your new identity in Christ?

7. As you recognize the spiritual battle, how can you rely on God's strength to take each thought captive and walk in obedience to Him?

Live It Out

1. **Prayer journal:** Start a prayer journal. Write down your worries, prayers, and reflections. Revisit your entries to see how God has worked through your prayers and brought you peace.

2. **Thought inventory:** Create a "thought inventory" where you list your current thoughts and compare them against the qualities in Philippians 4:8. Actively replace negative thoughts with positive ones that align with God's truth.

3. **Spiritual battle plan:** Develop a plan that includes specific prayers, Scriptures, and affirmations to turn to when facing mental strongholds or negative thought patterns.

4. **Renewal commitment:** Commit to renewing your mind daily. Set aside time each day for prayer, Scripture reading, and meditating on God's Word. Reflect on how this transforms your thoughts and actions over time.

5. **Meditate on Scripture:** Focus on the following verses this week: Philippians 4:6–8, 2 Corinthians 10:3–5, Romans 12:2, Ephesians 4:22–24, John 8:32.

6. **Memorize Scripture:** Choose a meaningful verse from this chapter to commit to memory.

7. **Gratitude list:** End each day by writing down three things you are grateful for. Shifting your focus to gratitude helps redirect negative thoughts and foster joy.

Can I Pray for You?

Heavenly Father, Thank You for the way You wired our brains—giving us the ability to think, process, and respond to the world through the lens of Your design. You are the Master Creator. You know our frailties and how often we struggle with our thoughts, especially when it's hard to stay focused on what's true and right. Your Word reminds us that Your thoughts and ways are higher than ours. So, we come to You, laying down everything that draws us into anxiety and depression. Thank You for always being with us, for equipping us for this battle, and for surrounding us with family and friends who share truth and encouragement. Fill us with Your strength to stay in the fight, eyes fixed on You, knowing that even in our struggles, You are working for our good and Your glory. In Jesus' name, Amen.

Works Cited

[1] "Understanding Psychosis." *National Institute of Mental Health (NIMH)*, 2019, https://www.nimh.nih.gov/health/publications/understanding-psychosis. Accessed 3 June 2025.

[2] LeWine, Howard E.. "Understanding the Stress Response." *Harvard Health*, 3 Apr. 2024, https://www.health.harvard.edu/staying-healthy/understanding-the-stress-response. Accessed 3 June 2025.

[3] LeWine, Howard E. "Understanding the Stress Response." *Harvard Health*, 3 Apr. 2024, https://www.health.harvard.edu/staying-healthy/understanding-the-stress-response. Accessed 3 June 2025.

[4] Wiginton, Keri. "Physical Effects of Depression on the Brain." *WebMD*, 31 July 2020, https://www.webmd.com/depression/depression-physical-effects-brain. Accessed 3 June 2025.

[5] Wiginton, Keri. "Physical Effects of Depression on the Brain." *WebMD*, 31 July 2020, https://www.webmd.com/depression/depression-physical-effects-brain. Accessed 3 June 2025.

[6] Neuroscience News. "Depression Alters Brain Circuits, Heightening Negative Perception." *Neuroscience News*, 25 Oct. 2024, https://neurosciencenews.com/depression-amygdala-emotional-processing-27943/. Accessed 3 June 2025.

[7] Wiginton, Keri. "Physical Effects of Depression on the Brain." *WebMD*, 31 July 2020, https://www.webmd.com/depression/depression-physical-effects-brain. Accessed 3 June 2025.

[8] Neuroscience News. "Depression Alters Brain Circuits, Heightening Negative Perception." *Neuroscience News*, 25 Oct. 2024, https://neurosciencenews.com/depression-amygdala-emotional-processing-27943/. Accessed 3 June 2025.

[9] Wiginton, Keri. "Physical Effects of Depression on the Brain." *WebMD*, 31 July 2020, https://www.webmd.com/depression/depression-physical-effects-brain. Accessed 3 June 2025.

[10] Paraphrase of a concept from David D. Burns, *Feeling Good: The New Mood Therapy*. Harper, 1980.

4

Your Past Matters

My Life Lesson

I didn't realize how much my past shaped my present until everything unraveled. During my days in psychosis, unexplainable anger and fear gripped me, and I didn't know why. It felt as though I was perpetually stuck in fight-or-flight mode. The anger simmered just below the surface and would often explode into harsh accusations against my husband. I became convinced he was planning either to divorce me or to harm me. The intensity of these emotions was terrifying.

In my delusional state, I constantly thought the worst was about to happen. That year, Steve surprised me with two dozen roses and a beautiful sapphire and diamond ring for our thirty-third anniversary. The gifts were characteristic of my thoughtful husband, but in my psychotic state, I immediately grew suspicious. What if the white gold band was really a toxic metal? My thoughts spiraled—once in contact with my skin, it would cause chronic health issues. I decided to wear the ring as little as possible. On the rare occasions when I wore it, fear quickly took over. I would slip it back into its box, out of sight, where it felt less threatening.

One evening, as Steve and I sat on the couch watching television, he noticed the ring wasn't on my finger. When he asked about it, I made up an excuse, claiming it didn't match my outfit. Ever mindful of the tension that had flared when I shared my thoughts months earlier, I was afraid to reveal the sinister path they had since taken. But that night, Steve continued to ask questions.

Scared to Be Alone

Crushing guilt from the two attempts to take my life, coupled with the overwhelming feeling that forgiveness was out of reach, drove me to the edge. I teetered there, afraid to push him too far, yet desperate to force his hand.

I don't remember the words I spoke, only the actions that followed. I went upstairs, got the symbolic ring from its box, and handed it to him. But I didn't stop there. I also removed my wedding ring and gave it to him. Shocked by my outburst, he mentioned putting them in safekeeping for a while and got up from the couch. Something inside me snapped. I ran after him, desperate to retrieve them.

In my distorted thinking, this felt like further proof that he was preparing to leave me. He now held the rings that symbolized our marriage. My thoughts collided with my deepest fear: *If he no longer wanted to be married to me, what would that mean for my future?*

Despite my harsh words and cruel actions that night, I didn't want my husband to leave—I still loved him. The thought of facing life alone was devastating. *What would I do without him? How would I survive?* I couldn't imagine trying to find a job after being out of the workforce for over twenty-five years. Everything felt like it was spinning out of control.

But reality couldn't have been further from my swirling thoughts. Steve never intended to leave. He continued to gently remind me of the truth, even as he wrestled with a difficult question: Was I capable of grasping the truth in my current state of mind, or was I simply unwilling to act on it?

Uncovering the Root

Conflict had been a trigger for me during my struggles with anxiety, depression, and psychosis, but it wasn't until after my healing that Steve and I uncovered the deeper cause. Growing up with an alcoholic dad, tension and confrontation were commonplace in our home. To avoid arguments, I followed the rules or steered conversations toward safe topics.

When disagreements escalated, usually between my older brother and dad, their voices rose, and tempers flared. My instinctive response was to shut down, emotionally withdrawing to protect myself. Over time, that pattern gradually shaped my thinking. I came to believe that staying quiet, hiding my emotions, and pretending everything was as it should be would keep me safe.

One evening, after a particularly intense argument, my dad warned me not to say a word about what had happened.

I was still allowed to go to a movie with a friend after dinner, but I dutifully kept my mouth shut. The angst I felt made me sick to my stomach, but I acted as if nothing was wrong. That night, I learned an unspoken rule: family dysfunction had to be hidden. It felt safer to maintain appearances than to speak the truth.

Facing Buried Anger

Although my dad stopped drinking by the time I was in high school, and we maintained an amicable relationship, the fear-based patterns I had developed remained. I didn't realize there were still unresolved issues buried beneath the surface.

Childhood trauma doesn't always involve the extremes like physical or sexual abuse. Sometimes, simply growing up in a home marked by conflict, fear, or emotional neglect can leave lasting wounds. Often, trauma is less about what happened and more about how our minds and hearts interpreted the experience, and whether we had the tools or support to process it.[1]

In my case, the emotions I had pushed down as a middle schooler eventually resurfaced decades later. I remember experiencing waves of anger during my first battle with anxiety and depression in 2006, when I was in my late thirties. For nine months, it seemed to wash over me with varying degrees of intensity. At the time, I was working with a Christian counselor, and I made a full recovery, but we never discovered the source of the anger.

Years later, when anxiety and depression returned with a vengeance, eventually spiraling into psychosis in 2023, that same feeling resurfaced, this time as full-blown rage. It confirmed an unsettling truth: I had carried the emotional patterns I learned in childhood into adulthood. Looking back, I can see many times when unprocessed pain from my youth triggered strong, intense responses later in life.

A trigger is often an instinctive response to something external—a sound, smell, word, or situation—that stirs up buried pain, sometimes without us fully understanding why.[2]

The Soundtrack That Played

The internal soundtrack of my childhood played on repeat: conflict was dangerous, and silence felt safe. It seemed easier to agree with others than risk creating waves. I became a people-pleaser.

When I entered psychosis, the internal soundtrack shifted. Disagreements still felt threatening, but I no longer sought to please people, as I had lost trust in everyone. Suspicion consumed me, and I second-guessed everyone's intentions. I relied solely on my judgment to determine what to do next.

I knew my irrational behavior was forcing my husband to make increasingly difficult decisions. He had stepped up my care, from sessions with a licensed therapist to appointments with a psychologist. If there wasn't a significant improvement, the next step would be admission to an inpatient mental health facility.

Despite Steve's relentless efforts to find help for me, I sabotaged each one. Out of fear, I lied to my psychologist and psychiatrist, convinced that if they knew the full extent of my thoughts, I'd be placed in residential care immediately. The soundtrack continued to play: *share just enough to satisfy, but keep the rest quiet.* I felt trapped. Home no longer felt like a safe haven, just a painful reminder of the tension I'd caused. Yet I was equally convinced that if I entered a facility, I would never get out.

I despised the person I had become, weighed down by guilt and shame like heavy garments I couldn't take off. The hostility I directed toward Steve and the few family members I still spoke to was a reflection of the anger I felt toward myself. Unable to excuse my actions, I convinced myself that forgiveness was out of reach—from my family, and especially from a holy God.

Breaking Free

But God had a far greater plan, and He never stopped pursuing me. Although the childhood trauma I experienced had shaped a dysfunctional response to conflict that resulted in mistrust, it couldn't stand against the power of His truth. In desperation, my husband called our pastor and his wife, along with four other couples—friends from our church— to come to our home, share God's Word, and pray with me. The gathering was more than a visit from supportive friends; it was *The Day of Truth.*

That day marked the first time I openly confessed that I had attempted to take my life twice. I also voiced a haunting fear: my actions proved I wasn't truly a child of God. The love and compassion shown by everyone who gathered that day opened my eyes to the forgiveness and hope available to me, despite my past actions.

Although past wounds had distorted my perspective, the apostle John's powerful words reminded me: "But if we walk in the light, as he is in the light, we have fellowship one with another, and the blood of Jesus Christ his Son cleanseth us from all sin" (1 John 1:7).

When I finally allowed God's light to shine on what I had worked so hard to keep hidden, the cycle of darkness was broken. It was a pivotal step toward healing. By God's grace and with my husband's help, we uncovered the childhood trauma I had long buried, opening the door for restoration to begin.

Maybe you've been carrying hidden pain too, buried wounds that continue to shape your responses to life and relationships. God sees it all, and His grace is greater. Let His light shine into the hidden places of your heart, inviting both healing and wholeness.

The Science Behind It

Our mind is fascinating. Designed by our Heavenly Father, it is a gift capable of remarkable creativity. We're able to compose symphonies, write stories, and paint masterpieces that resonate deeply with others.

It is also a powerful tool, helping us solve complex problems and make advances in technology. One of the most incredible aspects of our mind is its ability to experience a wide range of emotions: joy, sadness, anger, fear, excitement, envy, love, and compassion, to name a few.

It's astonishing to realize that only about ten percent of our thought process is on the conscious surface. Our subconscious mind is responsible for approximately ninety percent of our decision-making.[3] Christian theology and scientific research agree on the existence of the subconscious mind and its significant role in our lives.

Beneath the Surface: How the Subconscious Shapes Us

The Bible often uses the word *heart* interchangeably when referring to the mind. The renowned American philosopher and Christian theologian Dallas Willard explains it this way:

> The heart as Jesus uses it and as Christian theology uses it is not limited to the conscious mind alone but actually mostly the unconscious mind. The word "kardia" is translated to mean the heart; mind, character, inner self, will, intention, center. It means the "seat and center of all physical and spiritual life and the vigor and sense of physical life." It is also presented as the "seat of the thoughts, passions, desires, appetites, affections, purposes, endeavors."[4]

So, what is the subconscious or unconscious mind? Willard says:

> The subconscious, or unconscious mind, makes decisions without us being aware or having to think about them first. Our subconscious mind is like a bank full of memories, skills, beliefs, previous experiences, and everything that has ever happened to us. The capacity for our subconscious is practically unlimited. The unconscious mind affects our fears, what motivates us, our temperaments and attitudes, and our autonomic nervous system, which maintains balance in the billions of cells in our body.[5]

This vast storage space influences our behavior, emotions, and thoughts, often without our conscious awareness.

- **Behavior:** The subconscious mind controls habitual behaviors and automatic reactions. For example, when you brush your teeth or drive a familiar route, you rely on your subconscious to perform these tasks without conscious effort.[6]

- **Emotions:** Emotions often come from our subconscious, influenced by past experiences and memories. One of your senses might trigger a memory and bring up a strong emotional response, even if you can't pinpoint why (e.g. a smell, a song, a food, a location).[7]

- **Thoughts:** The subconscious mind shapes our thought patterns through ingrained beliefs and perceptions. These subconscious influences can affect how we interpret events, make decisions, and interact with others.[8]

Every experience in your life, stored in your subconscious, contributes to the continuous soundtrack of your mind, a combination of both the good and the bad. If the loudest soundtrack is negative, it will inevitably affect your mood, shape your attitude, and strain your relationships.

When trauma occurs early in life, as it did in mine, it has far-reaching effects. It has the power to cloud our thoughts, emotions, and behaviors, leading to unhealthy responses to future difficulties we face.

When the Brain Gets Stuck

Our brain tends to create ingrained patterns of thinking and behavior, which are often referred to as "ruts," under certain circumstances. Two key circumstances include:

- **Repetition:** When we repeatedly think or do something in the same way, neural pathways in our brain become more established, making it easier to continue that pattern.

- **Stress and anxiety:** Under stress or anxiety, our brains tend to revert to familiar patterns as a coping mechanism. This can result in negative thinking or behavior loops that are hard to break.[9]

The Brain's Built-In Healing Process

Since a significant portion of our brain activity occurs subconsciously, transforming negative thought patterns into positive ones requires considerable effort. The key is to identify the root cause of the negative thought pattern. There may be underlying trauma that needs to be uncovered and addressed to break the cycle. The good news is that healing is possible.

Amazingly, God created our brains with the capability to "recategorize information and rewire existing pathways so that changes in thought patterns, life routines, daily habits, and even addictive appetites are never impossible to recalibrate."[10] This process is known as *neuroplasticity*.

Overcoming a negative thought pattern can feel incredibly challenging, but God equips us with the ability to do so through the miraculous way He designed our brains. By replacing negative, faulty thoughts with truth and consistently practicing this new pattern, the neural pathways in our brain are rewired. We're equipped to embrace a healthier thought process and leave the old struggle behind.

Help and Hope from God's Word

We live in a fallen world, and sin makes it impossible for us to have a pain-free life. The immediate consequences of sin became evident following Adam and Eve's disobedience (Genesis 3:16–24):

- Separation from God
- Introduction of sin and death
- Cursed ground and hard work
- Pain in childbirth
- Conflict and strife
- Moral awareness and shame

Can you imagine the thoughts racing through their minds? The fractured relationships, with God and with each other? The endless "if only" scenarios replaying in their heads as they struggled to fall asleep? The mental soundtracks that had already begun to take hold?

The Perfect Plan

God had the perfect plan to pay the price for their sin. He sent His Son, Jesus, to take on human form, live a sinless life, and endure a cruel death on the cross. He shed His blood so they could be free. Why did He do this? Because He loved them. But His plan wasn't just for them; it was for all humanity: "For God so loved the world, that he gave his only begotten Son, that whosoever believeth in him should not perish, but have everlasting life" (John 3:16).

When we accept His gift of salvation, everything changes—our relationship with God, our eternal destiny, and the course of our entire life. Paul describes this transformation beautifully: "Therefore if any man be in Christ, he is a new creature: old things are passed away; behold, all things are become new" (2 Corinthians 5:17).

What an amazing transformation! In his earlier letter to the Corinthians, Paul shared a profound truth: "...we have the mind of Christ" (1 Corinthians 2:16). This truth still applies today. As believers, we have access to the Lord's understanding: His thoughts, His discernment, and His perfect plans. So, why do we still struggle with unhealthy thought patterns after salvation? Because we still live in a body of flesh, with minds shaped by past experiences and the coping mechanisms we've learned along the way.

The Holy Spirit's Role

At salvation, the Lord gives us His Holy Spirit to help us live in a way that honors Him. Here are a few of the roles the Holy Spirit fulfills in our lives:

- **Comforter:** offering us peace and consolation during life's challenges
- **Teacher:** guiding us in understanding and applying God's Word
- **Convicter:** revealing sin, righteousness, and judgment to align us with God's will
- **Sealer:** marking us as a child of God and securing our salvation
- **Intercessor:** praying on our behalf according to God's will

- **Empowerer:** strengthening us to live godly lives and share Christ's message with others

Through the Holy Spirit, we are empowered to renew the way our minds function. David penned the following heartfelt words: "Search me, O God, and know my heart: try me, and know my thoughts: And see if there be any wicked way in me, and lead me in the way everlasting" (Psalm 139:23–24). When we invite the Lord to search our deepest thoughts, the Holy Spirit reveals areas we need to confront, seek forgiveness for, and replace with His truth.

The Process of Renewal

When we allow the Lord to reveal the hidden things, both those we've intentionally concealed and those we're unaware of, He gives us the wisdom and strength to change and be renewed. This daily process requires time, but it's time well spent. The Lord is pleased when we seek Him and pursue the truth: "Behold, thou desirest truth in the inward parts: and in the hidden part thou shalt make me to know wisdom" (Psalm 51:6).

Picture the young shepherd, David, tending his father's sheep by day and protecting them from predators at night. In those quiet hours, he spent countless moments meditating on the Scripture he knew and reflecting deeply on God's character. Those experiences would later inspire him, through the guidance of the Holy Spirit, to compose many of the Psalms. Consider these verses:

Wherewithal shall a young man cleanse his way? by taking heed thereto according to thy word.

With my whole heart have I sought thee: O let me not wander from thy commandments.

Thy word have I hid in mine heart, that I might not sin against thee.

Blessed art thou, O Lord: teach me thy statutes.

With my lips have I declared all the judgments of thy mouth.

I have rejoiced in the way of thy testimonies, as much as in all riches.

I will meditate in thy precepts, and have respect unto thy ways.

I will delight myself in thy statutes: I will not forget thy word.

—Psalm 119:9–16

David clearly understood the importance of filling his heart with the Word of God. Despite his flaws and failures, the posture of David's heart and his relentless pursuit of God were beautiful. He was, after all, described as a man after God's own heart. We, too, can be known by this description when we surrender our thoughts to the gentle prompting of the Spirit, partner with Him to rewire and renew our minds, seek Christ wholeheartedly, and treasure His Word in our hearts.

 ## Your Turn: Reflection Questions and Action Steps

Pause and Reflect

1. Have you experienced unresolved emotions from your childhood that continue to affect your adult

life, especially during times of conflict or stress? If so, how are you managing them?

2. Have you ever noticed how your subconscious mind influences your daily decisions and behavior? Can you think of a specific instance where this happened?

3. How have past experiences or memories triggered strong emotional responses in your life? Are there specific triggers you have identified?

4. What negative thought patterns or behaviors have you recognized in your own life? How might God's design of the brain, through neuroplasticity, help you address these limiting beliefs?

5. How has receiving God's gift of salvation transformed your relationship with Him and shaped your daily life?

6. How does inviting the Lord to search your heart and examine what's hidden contribute to your spiritual growth and renewal?

7. What lessons can you draw from David's commitment to meditating on God's Word, and how can you apply these lessons to deepen your relationship with God?

Live It Out

1. **Identify and address triggers:** Take time to reflect on your life. Are there any unresolved childhood experiences or wounds that could be triggering negative emotions or responses today?

If so, consider seeking professional support to address these issues and develop healthier coping mechanisms.

2. **Notice harmful patterns:** Reflect on your thoughts, emotions, and behaviors. Acknowledge any unhealthy patterns or beliefs that may influence your daily life.

3. **Replace faulty thinking with God's truth:** Consciously practice replacing negative thoughts with truth-filled ones. This may involve daily affirmations and cultivating a mindset of gratitude.

4. **Engage your brain's God-given ability to rewire and heal:** Explore how God designed your brain to change and recover through neuroplasticity. Be intentional about activities that strengthen your mind and focus on His truth. For example: "When you wake up, instead of reaching for your phone, reach for your Bible. When you say something you regret—instead of criticizing yourself, embrace the opportunity to practice honest communication and healthy conflict."[11]

5. **Embrace salvation and transformation:** If you haven't already accepted God's gift of salvation through Jesus Christ, prayerfully consider it. It's the beginning of a restored relationship with God and a changed life. (See Appendix B for more information.)

6. **Invite the Holy Spirit to guide you:** Regularly invite the Holy Spirit to search your heart and mind, and to show you areas that need transformation. Ask for His guidance, comfort, and wisdom today.

7. **Engage with Scripture:** Make it a habit to read and meditate on God's Word. Just as David hid God's Word in his heart, seek to understand and apply biblical truth in your life. As you do, your thoughts and actions will align more closely with His will.

Can I Pray for You?

Heavenly Father, We stand in awe of the incredible gift of our minds—designed with creativity and filled with boundless potential. Thank You for the ability to experience a wide range of emotions. Help us honor You as we express them. Lord, we need Your guidance in transforming our thought patterns. Please bring to light any hidden wounds from our past that may be influencing our present. Search our hearts, O God, and reveal anything that needs Your healing touch. Give us strength to replace negative thoughts with Your truth and to embrace the amazing way You designed our brains to heal and renew. Father, thank You for the gift of Your Son, Jesus Christ, whose sacrifice brings us freedom and transformation. Help us to live as new creations, fully embracing the mind of Christ. May Your Holy Spirit guide, comfort, and empower us to honor You with our lives. Lead us in Your ways and fill us with Your wisdom. Just as David meditated on Your Word, help us to delight in it and to hide it in our hearts. Thank You for Your unwavering love and the hope we find as we walk in Your light. Help us grow in faith and draw closer to You each day. In Jesus' name, Amen.

Works Cited

1   Paraphrase of a concept from Diane Langberg, *Suffering and the Heart of God: How Trauma Destroys and Christ Restores*. New Growth Press, 2015.

2   Broom, Beth. "What Are Trauma Triggers?" *Christian Trauma Healing Network*, 7 Mar. 2022, https://christiantraumahealingnetwork. org/2022/03/common-trauma-triggers/. Accessed 1 July 2025.

3   Colon, Michael. "A Subconscious Insight into the Mind of the Spirit." *Katy Christian Magazine*, 23 Nov. 2022, https:// katychristianmagazine.com/2022/11/23/a-subconscious-insight-into-the-mind-of-the-spirit/. Accessed 30 June 2025.

4   Acha, Kenneth. "The Unconscious Mind in Christian Theology." *Servants University: Training Servants for Christ*, 5 Mar. 2017, https://www.servantsuniversity.com/the-unconscious-mind-in-christian-theology/. Accessed 30 June 2025.

5   Colon, Michael. "A Subconscious Insight into the Mind of the Spirit." *Katy Christian Magazine*, 23 Nov. 2022, https:// katychristianmagazine.com/2022/11/23/a-subconscious-insight-into-the-mind-of-the-spirit/. Accessed 30 June 2025.

6   Gibson, E. D. "How the Subconscious Influences Our Daily Habits and Routines." *Medium*, 27 Sept. 2024, https://deconch30.medium.com/how-the-subconscious-influences-our-daily-havits-and-routines-5e4368e87042. Accessed 30 June 2025.

7   Kellemen, Bob. "21 Resources on a Biblical View of Our Emotions." *RPM Ministries*, 11 Dec. 2023, https://rpmministries.org/2023/12/21-free-resources-about-our-emotions-and-the-bible/. Accessed 1 July 2025.

8   Pope, Pamela. "Breaking Negative Thought Patterns." *Seattle Christian Counseling*, 14 Nov. 2022, https://seattlechristiancounseling.com/articles/breaking-negative-thought-patterns. Accessed 1 July 2025.

9   Andersen, Kayla. "Brain Science and the Bible: How God's Design for Neural Pathways Brings Hope." *Take It from Kayla*, 11 Nov. 2022, https://takeitfromkayla.com/brain-science-and-the-bible/. Accessed 1 July 2025.

10   Andersen, Kayla. "Brain Science and the Bible: How God's Design for Neural Pathways Brings Hope." *Take It from Kayla*, 11 Nov. 2022, https://takeitfromkayla.com/brain-science-and-the-bible/. Accessed 1 July 2025.

11   Andersen, Kayla. "Brain Science and the Bible: How God's Design for Neural Pathways Brings Hope." *Take It from Kayla*, 11 Nov. 2022, https://takeitfromkayla.com/brain-science-and-the-bible/. Accessed 1 July 2025.

5

Find Your People—Be Open and Honest

My Life Lesson

Friendship has always held a special place in my life. I treasure moments spent with friends—catching up on life, taking a walk together, or sharing prayer requests over the phone. The bond that forms and deepens through these simple connections is life-giving.

When anxiety and depression took hold in 2021, I didn't recognize the shift at first. But over time, the need to hide what I was going through began to outweigh my desire to stay connected. Shame and embarrassment silenced me, isolating me in fear and hopelessness.

I agonized over what others must be thinking, imagining the worst. They probably noticed my awkward behavior and wondered why I was no longer attending the ladies' events. The longer my thoughts stayed on a negative path, the more they unraveled.

Initially, Steve thought my behavior was due to a lack of confidence, given my struggles to lead a book study with a group of women. But as I gradually withdrew from other responsibilities and then begged him to step away from the Sunday School class we had taught for years, he realized this went far deeper than insecurity, and it was only getting worse.

At the same time, I was pulling back from my commitments and quietly distancing myself from friends. Invitations were met with either excuses or vague, non-committal responses. Steve picked up on the disconnection and did his best to help me re-engage. When I met his suggestions with resistance, he arranged for friends to stop by, inviting me to go for a walk in our neighborhood, anything to get me to interact again. Like an obstinate child, the harder he tried, the more I pushed back.

Unwilling to give up, he encouraged me to schedule an appointment with a Christian therapist so I could receive the care I needed. But when the sessions didn't bring immediate relief, and my symptoms persisted, I found it increasingly difficult to connect, not only with friends but even with my husband.

The Struggle to Open Up

When I ran out of excuses and had to attend an event, I used Steve as a human shield. As long as he was with me, I could stay in the background, letting him speak for both of us and deflecting any uncomfortable questions that might come my way.

I remember one evening in particular: we attended a concert at my friend Shannon's farm, where teenagers from our church were performing. Steve was running the sound system for the singers, so I couldn't take up my usual place at his side. I was visibly distraught.

Sensing something was wrong, Shannon sat down across from me and asked directly what was going on. Her pointed question left me with no place to hide. So I told her the truth. I was battling anxiety and depression.

In the weeks that followed, Shannon made time in her busy schedule to stop by, giving us a chance to talk. My responses were often brief, and I would quickly redirect the conversation away from myself, shifting the focus to safer, less threatening topics. Opening up felt extremely uncomfortable. I was afraid of being seen as weak, or worse, unspiritual. The shame I felt made it nearly impossible to be honest, even with people I trusted.

The longer I grappled with anxiety and depression, the harder it became to talk about what I was going through. Having overcome these challenges before, I couldn't understand why I couldn't shake the symptoms this time. Admitting that I was battling persistent negative thoughts felt humiliating, especially since I had once written and taught a course on transforming negative thought patterns.

Facing the same struggle again felt like failure. My thoughts, born of fear and shame, gradually gained ground. Instead of replacing the lies with truth, I let them take root. Depression added to the weight by whispering an even darker lie: I wasn't just failing—I *was* a failure.

Pride, Guilt, and Shame
Blinded by pride, I refused to admit I needed help. I was more preoccupied with how others perceived me than with

being honest about my struggles and taking steps toward freedom. Yet, throughout my two-and-a-half-year trial, my friends continued to reach out to me, calling, texting, sending cards, and notes of encouragement. Sometimes, I would respond, pretending nothing was wrong, but more often, I didn't respond at all.

After the first attempt to end my life, communication became even more strained. The guilt and shame were crushing. *How had I ended up here?* I wanted nothing more than to erase my mistakes and return to the life I had before anxiety and depression descended. I convinced myself that ignoring it all would make the regret and humiliation fade, but instead, they only grew louder.

On warm evenings, Steve often encouraged me to join him in our screen room, hoping the peaceful setting would lead to meaningful conversation. Instead, I focused on superficial topics, like the weather and our pets. At the time, I didn't realize I was desperately trying to avoid any conflict, trapped by the unprocessed hurt of my childhood.

Even the therapist I saw at the time wasn't able to break through to me. Since I refused to share my true thoughts, our sessions remained one-sided. She encouraged me to journal, paint, and stay curious, but most sessions uncovered the same two emotions: guilt and shame—my constant companions.

A Second Attempt

I convinced myself that Steve had asked my friends to stay in touch with me. In my distorted thinking, I believed they were only reaching out to report my odd behavior back to him. By November of 2022, things had reached a crossroads. Over dinner, Steve gently encouraged me to renew my friendships and consider stepping back into some form of ministry. The thought alone filled me with alarm. Pretending to be fine had already taken every bit of my strength. I was certain that if I re-engaged with people, they would see the mess inside and reject me.

The painful reality was that I had rejected myself. I saw myself as broken beyond repair, unworthy of love, and undeserving of the very grace I had once so confidently taught others.

Within days of that conversation, I made a second attempt to take my life. Only a handful of people knew: my husband, our daughter, son-in-law, my mom, my brother, and my therapist. We were advised not to inform the medical community, as having a second suicide attempt on record would have significant repercussions.

From that point on, communication came to a standstill. Additional layers of guilt and shame settled on me, driving me deeper into the torment of my thoughts. Not long after, psychotic episodes began, and we stopped attending church.

For my husband, pretending that everything was fine became unbearable, especially when it was far from the truth. He found strength in surrounding himself with friends who supported and encouraged him. I went in the opposite direction, cutting off ties with friends until I was completely isolated.

Survival Mode

I refused to listen to anything Steve said, convinced I knew better. All I wanted to do was argue, spewing ugly words meant to attack and wound. Yet, by God's grace, Steve continued to respond with love. He challenged me with the truth of God's Word, continued to search for the right treatment plan to help me move forward, and forgave me even when I was anything but cooperative.

Caught in survival mode, I became a habitual liar—hiding the truth from everyone around me: my husband, family, doctors, and friends. I had already shared enough irrational thoughts to realize they weren't being taken seriously, or kindly. So, I told people what I thought they wanted to hear, pretending to agree with their advice while silently battling overwhelming inner turmoil. Terrified I'd be institutionalized, I buried the truth even deeper.

My brief stay in a behavioral health hospital after the first suicide attempt had left a lasting impact. Recognizing how harmful it had been, my husband did everything in his power to keep me at home. However, as my behavior became increasingly difficult to manage, he quickly found himself running out of options. The only path forward seemed to be an inpatient treatment center.

Honesty and Love

Keeping my struggle hidden only intensified the internal war I was already fighting. Thankfully, God's grace prevailed. In August 2023, on what we now call *The Day of Truth*, I finally opened up to my friends about my two suicide attempts and the pain my actions had caused. The battle began to lose its power that day. It felt good to have everything out in the open. A profound sense of relief followed. There were no more secrets.

Open communication with my husband and friends marked the beginning of my healing journey. The wounds I experienced as a child instilled a deep sense of mistrust—both toward my husband and, ultimately, my Heavenly Father—making it difficult to share my darkest thoughts and feelings.

Though I couldn't see it then, Steve had always been fighting for me. The unconditional love he and my friends showed reflected their genuine care.

It is a privilege to be surrounded by people who love us enough to correct us when we're wrong, challenge our thinking, and speak God's truth into our lives. Don't underestimate the power of honesty. Choose to be open and transparent with those you trust.

The Science Behind It

From the very beginning, God designed us to thrive in relationships, as we see in the book of Genesis: "And the Lord God said, It is not good that the man should be alone; I will make him an help meet for him" (Genesis 2:18).

Companionship, whether in marriage or friendship, is part of God's design for us. Researchers have found that close relationships play a vital role in our overall well-being. Friends not only help us celebrate life's milestones, but they also offer encouragement during challenging times. They build a sense of belonging, helping us resist the pull of isolation and loneliness. The benefits of friendship include:

- Increasing our sense of connection and purpose
- Boosting our happiness and reducing stress
- Enhancing our self-confidence and feelings of self-worth
- Helping us navigate difficult seasons
- Encouraging us to change or avoid unhealthy habits[1]

Strong companionship also has a notable impact on our physical health. According to the Mayo Clinic, "Adults with strong social connections have a lower risk of many health problems. That includes depression, high blood pressure and an unhealthy weight. In fact, studies have found that older adults who have close friends and healthy social supports are likely to live longer than do their peers who have fewer friends."[2]

The Pull Toward Isolation

These insights offer a compelling case for cultivating meaningful friendships. But I learned firsthand that building relationships can be complicated when you're dealing with anxiety and depression. Several underlying factors can drive the tendency to withdraw. Research points to several key reasons why this happens:

- **Avoiding stress:** We may isolate ourselves to avoid the overwhelm of connecting with others. While this might bring short-term relief, avoidance often reinforces the anxiety, creating a cycle that's difficult to break.[3]
- **Feeling misunderstood:** We might think that others don't understand our struggles or that we're a

burden to family and friends. This kind of thinking can lead to withdrawal as a way of self-protection from perceived rejection or judgment.[4]

- **Low energy and motivation:** Depression can leave us drained, both emotionally and physically, making it difficult to reach out. The effort required to engage with others can feel impossible to manage.[5]

- **Negative self-perception:** Anxiety and depression can distort our self-image. We may start to feel that we're unworthy of friendship or that others don't enjoy our company. These lies can lead to self-imposed isolation.[6]

- **Compounding effects of loneliness:** Isolation can intensify the symptoms of depression and anxiety, creating a vicious cycle. Loneliness intensifies feelings of hopelessness and despair, making it even harder to break the pattern.[7]

Steps to Reconnect

Breaking the cycle of isolation can be challenging, but it's possible with the right support system and strategies. For me, it meant trusting my husband; being open and honest with my friends, family, and medical professionals; uncovering the root cause of my anxiety and depression; and choosing to trust God and His plan for my life instead of clinging to control. Other strategies may also include the following:

- **Therapy and counseling:** Engaging with a mental health professional can provide guidance and support.[8]

- **Peer support groups:** Gradual exposure to safe social situations can help rebuild confidence.[9]
- **Routine and structure:** Creating a regular schedule that includes social connections can make interaction feel more natural and reduce loneliness.[10]
- **Relaxation techniques:** Practices like progressive muscle relaxation can help manage anxiety symptoms and reduce the fear of interacting with others.[11]

The Healing Power of Friendship

Once the cycle of isolation is broken, friendship becomes a lifeline of support. Speaking with honesty and transparency paves the way for personal well-being and lasting connections. Some of the benefits include:

- **Improved relationships:** Honest communication builds trust and strengthens friendships, creating a safe space where individuals can share openly without fear of rejection.[12]
- **Better mental and emotional health:** Being truthful and transparent is linked to lower levels of stress and anxiety, as well as an increase in overall happiness.[13]
- **Reduced loneliness:** Stronger bonds with others reduce feelings of isolation and loneliness. The bond with others is significant for mental wellness.[14]

Are you struggling to connect with your friends? Have you pulled back from social activities you once enjoyed? Remember, you were created in the image of God, designed to thrive in relationships. Take a step today. Reach out to a trusted friend and share the thoughts and feelings that have been weighing you down.

Help and Hope from God's Word

Although the word *friendship* rarely appears in the Bible, its concept is woven throughout Scripture. The beautiful bond between David and Jonathan is a prime example worth examining more closely.

Jonathan, the son of King Saul and heir to Israel's throne, stood in stark contrast to David, the humble shepherd and musician from Bethlehem. Though they seemed unlikely friends with little in common, God had a unique plan for their relationship and the role they would play in each other's lives.

We aren't told exactly when David and Jonathan first met, but David spent considerable time at the palace. He had been chosen to play the harp to soothe King Saul, who was tormented by an evil spirit after disobeying God. David initially found favor with Saul, and the king even appointed him as his armor-bearer. But as David's victories in battle multiplied and God's favor became increasingly evident, jealousy took root in Saul's heart and began to grow.

Friendship and a Covenant

By the time David and Jonathan's friendship is recorded, David had already been secretly anointed as Israel's next king and was widely celebrated for his victory over Goliath. These were not the kind of circumstances that would typically spark a friendship with the crown prince, but the Lord was working out His plan:

And it came to pass, when he had made an end of speaking unto Saul, that the soul of Jonathan was knit with the soul of David, and Jonathan loved him as his own soul. And Saul took him that day, and would let him go no more home to his father's house. Then Jonathan and David made a covenant, because he loved him as his own soul. And Jonathan stripped himself of the robe that was upon him, and gave it to David, and his garments, even to his sword, and to his bow, and to his girdle.

—1 Samuel 18:1–4

Jonathan's Loyalty

Although he was next in line for the throne, Jonathan accepted that God's plan was for David to become Israel's next king. During challenging times, when his father, King Saul, sought to kill David, Jonathan courageously defended his friend's character and provided him with critical information, saving his life on multiple occasions.

The situation continued to escalate. At one point, David had to escape through a window to flee for his life. Saul's relentless pursuit showed no signs of stopping. Desperate for clarity, David turned to Jonathan for counsel. The two devised a test during the new moon feast: David would stay away, pretending to be ill, while Jonathan would observe Saul's response and determine whether his father truly intended to harm David.

A Second Sacred Promise

Another beautiful binding agreement was spoken:

And Jonathan said unto David, O Lord God of Israel, when I have sounded my father about to morrow any time, or the third day, and, behold, if there be good toward David, and I then send not unto thee, and shew it thee; The Lord do so and much more to Jonathan: but if it please my father to do thee evil, then I will shew it thee, and send thee away, that thou mayest go in peace: and the Lord be with thee, as he hath been with my father. And thou shalt not only while yet I live shew me the kindness of the Lord, that I die not: But also thou shalt not cut off thy kindness from my house for ever: no, not when the Lord hath cut off the enemies of David every one from the face of the earth.

—1 Samuel 20:12–15

According to the *Thomas Nelson King James Study Bible*:

Kindness and love are essential ingredients in the covenant stipulations of the ancient Near East. They speak of a relationship whereby each party treats the other as a full family member, with loyalty, dignity, and devotion. Jonathan continues with recognition of David's divinely established preeminence. The everlasting covenant between Jonathan and David will be remembered by David when he becomes king.[15]

After Jonathan's death, King David remained faithful to their sacred promise. He sought out Jonathan's remaining relatives to offer his support and discovered Mephibosheth, who had been lame since childhood. David welcomed him into his household, treating him like one of his sons and providing for him all his days.

Jesus: The Ultimate Friend

While Jonathan and David's story is an exceptional testimony of true friendship, the life of Jesus Christ stands as the ultimate example. He humbled Himself, sacrificing His life so we could be free: "Greater love hath no man than this, that a man lay down his life for his friends" (John 15:13).

Jesus embodies kindness, meekness, patience, forgiveness, holiness, and justice. He is the friend who sticks closer than a brother, the Everlasting Father who will never abandon us, and the One who speaks truth through His Word: "All scripture is given by inspiration of God, and is profitable for doctrine, for reproof, for correction, for instruction in righteousness" (2 Timothy 3:16).

We can model our friendships after these godly principles:

- Putting others first (Romans 12:10)
- Loving others (Galatians 5:14)
- Treating others as you want to be treated (Matthew 7:12)
- Treating others with kindness (Ephesians 4:32)
- Forgiving others (Colossians 3:13)
- Communicating truth in love (Ephesians 4:15)

God's Word emphasizes the blessings that come from building meaningful connections with others. Friendships create opportunities to give and receive love, support, and encouragement. Through life's highs and lows, these relationships draw us closer to one another and to God. We aren't meant to walk this journey alone, but to share it in community with friends.

 ## Your Turn: Reflection Questions and Action Steps

Pause and Reflect

1. Think of a time when a friend helped you through a difficult season. How did their support affect your mental and emotional health?

2. How might open and honest communication strengthen your relationships and support your emotional health?

3. What can you learn about loyalty and sacrifice from Jonathan's actions toward David, even knowing David would be king?

4. How does David's example of seeking Jonathan's counsel encourage you to seek advice from trusted friends and family?

5. How can you actively show love to your friends and family, fulfilling the commandment "Thou shalt love thy neighbour as thyself" (Galatians 5:14b)?

6. Recall a time when you experienced kindness and forgiveness in a friendship. How did it impact you?

7. How can you deepen your relationship with Jesus, the One who laid down His life for you?

Live It Out

1. **Identify and reach out to your people:** Make a list of family members and friends you trust and initiate a conversation with one person this week.

2. **Accept support from loved ones:** Allow family and friends to help you, and receive their encouragement and assistance.

3. **Practice open and honest communication:** As you continue to engage with family, friends, and medical professionals, commit to sharing your thoughts and feelings regularly to build trust and deepen connection.

4. **Seek wise counsel:** Be intentional about asking trusted loved ones for advice and feedback.

5. **Engage in regular activities:** Choose walking, a coffee date, or another activity with friends to maintain and strengthen your bonds, even when it's challenging.

6. **Cultivate a spirit of selflessness:** Put others first by prioritizing your friends' well-being and supporting them on their journey.

7. **Stay connected during tough times:** Remain close to your loved ones, and be the kind of friend who offers emotional and spiritual support when they face difficulties.

Can I Pray for You?

Gracious Lord, Thank You for creating us to live in community with others. You designed us to build friendships, sharing one another's joys and bearing each other's burdens. Fill us with grace and strength as we follow Your plan. When anxious thoughts and depression cloud our minds, remind us to reach out—first to You, and then to those who know and love us. We need Your help to be open and honest about the struggles we're facing. Your Word is full of examples of Your people crying out to You and pouring out their thoughts and emotions. You invited them to cast their cares on You, because You could handle it all. Thank You for listening to us as well and replacing our chaos with Your peace. Forgive us when pride keeps us from admitting our need, and when we pretend nothing is wrong. Our friends are a blessing. Give us the courage to share our struggles with those we trust and to accept their direction, assistance, and encouragement. Give us the wisdom to recognize when we need support beyond what they can offer. Help us be the kind of friend who puts others first and is available in their time of need. No matter the challenges we both face, give us the perseverance to remain loyal, offering emotional and spiritual support as we grow in our relationship. Thank You for the gift of friendship. In Jesus' name, Amen.

Works Cited

1   "Friendships: Enrich Your Life and Improve Your Health." *Mayo Clinic*, 2024, https://www.mayoclinic.org/healthy-lifestyle/adult-health/in-depth/friendships/art-20044860. Accessed 10 July 2025.

2   "Friendships: Enrich Your Life and Improve Your Health." *Mayo Clinic*, 2024, https://www.mayoclinic.org/healthy-lifestyle/adult-health/in-depth/friendships/art-20044860. Accessed 10 July 2025.

3   Novotney, Amy. "The Risks of Social Isolation." *American Psychological Association*, 2019, https://www.apa.org/monitor/2019/05/ce-corner-isolation. Accessed 10 July 2025.

4   Novotney, Amy. "The Risks of Social Isolation." *American Psychological Association*, 2019, https://www.apa.org/monitor/2019/05/ce-corner-isolation. Accessed 10 July 2025.

5   Novotney, Amy. "The Risks of Social Isolation." *American Psychological Association*, 2019, https://www.apa.org/monitor/2019/05/ce-corner-isolation. Accessed 10 July 2025.

6   Kolonko, Catherine. "How Does Self-Esteem Relate to Depression." *Psych Central*, 14 Apr. 2022, https://psychcentral.com/depression/is-low-self-esteem-making-you-vulnerable-to-depression. Accessed 10 July 2025.

7   Novotney, Amy. "The Risks of Social Isolation." *American Psychological Association*, 2019, https://www.apa.org/monitor/2019/05/ce-corner-isolation. Accessed 10 July 2025.

8   NeuroLaunch Editorial Team. "Self-Isolating Behavior: Causes, Effects, and Coping Strategies." *NeuroLaunch*, 22 Sept. 2024, https://neurolaunch.com/self-isolating-behavior. Accessed 10 July 2025.

9   NeuroLaunch Editorial Team. "Self-Isolating Behavior: Causes, Effects, and Coping Strategies." *NeuroLaunch*, 22 Sept. 2024, https://neurolaunch.com/self-isolating-behavior. Accessed 10 July 2025.

10   Plata, Mariana. "The Power of Routines in Your Mental Health." *Psychology Today*, 4 Oct. 2018, https://www.psychologytoday.com/us/blog/the-gen-y-psy/201810/the-power-of-routines-in-your-mental-health. Accessed 10 July 2025.

11   NeuroLaunch Editorial Team. "Self-Isolating Behavior: Causes, Effects, and Coping Strategies." *NeuroLaunch*, 22 Sept. 2024, https://neurolaunch.com/self-isolating-behavior. Accessed 10 July 2025.

12   Le, Bonnie M., et al. "When the Truth Helps and When It Hurts: How Honesty Shapes Well-Being." *Current Opinion in Psychology*, vol. 46, June 2022, p. 101397, https://doi.org/10.1016/j.copsyc.2022.101397. Accessed 10 July 2025.

13   Le, Bonnie M., et al. "When the Truth Helps and When It Hurts: How Honesty Shapes Well-Being." *Current Opinion in Psychology*, vol. 46,

June 2022, p. 101397, https://doi.org/10.1016/j.copsyc.2022.101397. Accessed 10 July 2025.

[14] NeuroLaunch Editorial Team. "Self-Isolating Behavior: Causes, Effects, and Coping Strategies." *NeuroLaunch*, 22 Sept. 2024, https://neurolaunch.com/self-isolating-behavior. Accessed 10 July 2025.

[15] *The King James Study Bible, Full-Color Edition: Holy Bible, King James Version*. Edited by Thomas Nelson, Thomas Nelson Incorporated, 2017, p. 508-509.

Part 3:

Your Spirit

6

Read for Renewal

My Life Lesson

A typical morning for me begins with reading a few chapters of the Bible, recording what God has shown me, and spending time in prayer. I'm inspired by various reading plans, whether chronological, historical, or thematic. Regardless of which plan I follow, God's Word remains alive and active, designed to draw me closer to Him and deepen my relationship with Him.

When anxiety resurfaced in the spring of 2021, my routine didn't change right away. I continued to read and pray, but I struggled to stay focused. Sitting in the screen room with the Bible open on my lap, the sound of the creek murmuring in our front yard should have been calming. During that season, however, the creek's peaceful gurgle was often drowned out by distant sirens. Living near the hospital made them a common occurrence. *Why had I never noticed it before?*

I equated the shrill sound with distress and felt my heart skip a beat. An ambulance meant someone was in danger, someone who was no longer in control. As the scenarios played out in my mind, and I acknowledged my own exhaustion, I let the next anxious thought linger: *Soon I'll be out of control, too.* My lack of focus shifted to panic. It was difficult to pull myself back into the present. The usual peace I experienced from time spent with the Lord was slowly replaced by an unsettling fear.

Trying to Fix What Felt Broken

I automatically assumed there was a spiritual problem when the waves of anxiety and depression came crashing down. I didn't stop to consider the possibility of underlying physical or emotional factors. Years earlier, I faced similar mental struggles and uncovered lies I believed, so this time, I assumed I must have missed something. *Surely, I wouldn't be feeling this bad unless there was something more to uncover.* That mindset marked the beginning of a downward spiral.

I latched onto anything I might have done wrong, searching for a reason behind what I was experiencing. Even though I knew God was good, I wrestled with why He was allowing me to go through this a second time. The sense of being out of control escalated. My reaction was one of self-protection: try to fix the problem while earning back God's favor.

Through it all, Steve was incredibly understanding with me. He gently talked me through my illogical thought patterns, communicating God's truth with clarity and compassion. But instead of seeing the situation as a trial that could produce something valuable in my life, I simply wanted it to end.

Drifting Away from God

As my anxiety increased over the next few months and a lack of sleep muddled my thinking, my morning quiet time blurred into a meaningless routine. I had to read passages numerous times just to make sense of them, only to forget their content a short time later. I could feel myself drifting away. What had once been a vibrant relationship with the Lord had dissolved into an empty ritual. As I withdrew, a growing sense of fear and mistrust took hold, leading me to question God's character.

Each day, I skimmed through the same chapters in the book of Psalms. *How could something I once cherished dissolve into nothing more than a dreaded task?* With a distorted perspective, I fixated on verses that amplified my fears while overlooking the ones that could have offered comfort and encouragement. In the process, I lost sight of my identity as a beloved child of God. Instead, I saw myself as His adversary, convinced of it because I could no longer sense His presence.

Several Psalms I read beautifully captured the human author's trouble and anguish as he cried out to God, followed by God's gracious response. Psalm 22 was just one of many powerful examples:

My God, my God, why hast thou forsaken me? why art thou so far from helping me, and from the words of my roaring?

O my God, I cry in the day time, but thou hearest not; and in the night season, and am not silent.

. . .

For he hath not despised nor abhorred the affliction of the afflicted; neither hath he hid his face from him; but when he cried unto him, he heard.

—Psalm 22:1–2, 24

Although my circumstances were vastly different from the Psalmist's—he was surrounded by physical enemies, while I was battling invisible ones: anxiety and depression— we were both facing profound challenges. Yet, these passages didn't lift my feelings of despair. I overlooked the truth that God doesn't look down on us in our suffering, nor does He turn His back on us.

My biggest mistake was failing to recognize His response to our cries: He hears us. Instead, I allowed myself to remain fixated on my problems.

Increasing Doubt

Doubts about my salvation began to surface. Over the next two years, Steve patiently shared the gospel with me more than a hundred times. Decades earlier, I had acknowledged I was a sinner in need of a Savior and believed that Jesus lived a perfect, sinless life, shed His blood, died on the cross to pay for my sins, was buried, and rose again three days later.

But now, no matter how many times I revisited those same Scripture verses, the misgivings persisted. The anxiety and depression didn't go away, and the cycle of doubt deepened. My distorted thoughts convinced me I was destined for hell.

The farther I drifted from the Lord, the more tangled my thought patterns became. Confusion dominated. In my delusional state, I did not realize it was a tactic of the enemy, the author of confusion (1 Corinthians 14:33). When I shut God out, I became an easy target. No longer able to stand against the countless lies of the enemy, I fell prey to their insidious poison. My negative thought spiral held me captive in relentless torment.

The Weight of Desperation

I was desperate for God to heal me. When He didn't, desperation morphed into despair and anger. The sense of hopelessness became so heavy that I did something I never thought I would do. I attempted to take my life, not once, but twice.

Now the anger I felt turned inward. I despised myself, and I took it out on the people I loved most.

Faced with the reality of my situation, shame consumed me. I couldn't let go of the false belief that *Christians don't attempt suicide.* I condemned myself and felt unworthy even to approach God. Unable to receive the hope and forgiveness His Word offered, I felt entirely cut off. I knew He was still there, but I loathed myself, convinced my heart had become too calloused for Him to reach. *Was there any other choice than for Him to abandon me to my destructive ways?*

The searing guilt and shame that followed those attempts made it nearly impossible for me to open my

Bible. All I could see on every page was judgment and condemnation. Though I knew the familiar promise of 1 John 1:9, "If we confess our sins, he is faithful and just to forgive us our sins, and to cleanse us from all unrighteousness," I could not apply it to myself. I felt my sin was beyond God's forgiveness.

Unconditional Love & Acceptance

The Lord used the unconditional love and acceptance shown by my husband, our pastor, and his wife, as well as several other couples from our church, to draw me back to His side. Their actions were a living demonstration of the truths found in His Word: bearing one another's burdens and sharing the truth in love. In the ashes of my heart, a spark of hope was reignited.

Looking back, I see unmistakable evidence of His presence throughout that season of intense struggle. He was there all along, inviting me back into close fellowship through the power of His Word.

The Science Behind It

The Bible is unlike any other book ever written. It is the inspired Word of God. The book of Second Peter puts it this way: "For the prophecy came not in old time by the will of man: but holy men of God spake as they were moved by the Holy Ghost" (2 Peter 1:21).

God's Word has the power to radically change lives: "For the word of God is quick, and powerful, and sharper than any twoedged sword, piercing even to the dividing asunder of soul and spirit, and of the joints and marrow, and is a discerner of the thoughts and intents of the heart" (Hebrews 4:12).

Struggling to Read God's Word

When you're struggling with anxiety and depression, even reading a book can be difficult. In my own experience, each of the following played a role:

- **Difficulty concentrating:** Both conditions can make it hard to focus, stay engaged, and understand the material.[1]
- **Low energy levels:** Depression often causes fatigue, making the effort to read feel overwhelming.[2]
- **Negative thought patterns:** Persistent negative thoughts can make it difficult to enjoy or absorb what you're reading.[3]
- **Lack of motivation:** Reading may feel unimportant or even pointless.[4]

Unfortunately, reading the Bible may present deeper challenges:

- **Feelings of worthlessness:** Anxiety and depression can lead to guilt and shame, convincing you that you are unworthy of God's love and attention.[5]
- **Spiritual confusion:** You may begin to question your faith or feel disconnected from God.[6]

Recognizing Guilt, Releasing Shame

Guilt and shame are powerful emotions often experienced by those suffering from anxiety and depression. But what's the difference between the two? And what impact do they have on us? Pastor Derek Russell offers a masterful explanation of the difference between guilt and shame:

To understand what shame is, it is helpful to understand what guilt is in contrast. Imagine a little child whose mother tells them not to reach into the cookie jar and have cookies before dinner. When the mother isn't looking, the child makes a beeline for the cookie jar and devours a couple of them. The child may instinctively have a feeling of remorse. They feel guilty. They would say, "I did something bad." But let's say the sense of what they have done goes even deeper. Let's say that their reaction is not just, "I did something bad," but "I am bad." That is shame. Shame steps beyond the line of healthy guilt into unhealthy feelings and beliefs of worthlessness. "Of course I took the cookies. I was powerless to do otherwise. I am bad right down to the core."[7]

He continues:

Guilt holds out the possibility that things can get better. "I can decide not to do the wrong thing anymore. I can make amends for what I have done wrong. I can change my behavior in the future because I don't want to be guilty anymore. I can be forgiven." Shame is a web that is hard to escape from. Shame reinforces itself. "I can't do any better in the future. I am a lost cause. Because I am bad, I will screw up the next time too!"[8]

Russell's conclusion is powerful and worth noting:

Belief drives behavior. What you believe about yourself, your own identity, largely determines how you will act in the future. If someone internalizes feelings of shame, the shame becomes a self-fulfilling prophecy. Shame grows in secrecy, silence, and judgment. If you have a pervading sense of shame and are engaging in behavior that is wrong, shame makes you want to hide it (think about Adam and Eve trying to cover up their nakedness, or King David murdering Uriah to cover up his adultery). Shame thrives in the darkness, and in order to disarm it, it needs to be brought out into the light.[9]

Step Into the Light

If you're finding it difficult to read the Bible right now, take a moment to consider your view of God as well as your view of yourself. Remember, His Word is alive and active, revealing what lies at the core of your heart. Is there guilt from wrongdoing that needs to be confessed? Is shame keeping you silent?

Let God meet you there. Talk to Him honestly about what you're wrestling with and share it with a trusted friend. Shame begins to lose its grip the moment it's brought into the light.

Help and Hope from God's Word

It can't be overstated: God's Word is powerful. It reveals who God is, offering beautiful glimpses of His character, while also showing us who we are—deeply flawed human beings, yet radically loved by our Creator.

When my struggle was most intense, I stopped reading the Bible. I felt too weighed down by guilt and shame. But God continued pursuing me. The story of Jonah is a powerful reminder that even when we run from Him, He never abandons us. It's one of many places in Scripture where His mercy is on full display.

Jonah: A Story of Reluctance and Pursuit

Jonah's account is one of the best-known in the Bible. I remember hearing the story as a child. You probably did, too. But it's much more than a tale about a man swallowed by a big fish. The story offers a close-up look at God's patience and compassion, not only for His reluctant prophet but also for the people of a wicked nation unaware of Him.

The Lord instructed him to go to the city of Nineveh and warn its people that they would be destroyed in forty days if they didn't repent of their sins. Just three short verses into the book, we read his response: "But Jonah rose up to flee unto Tarshish from the presence of the Lord, and went down to Joppa; and he found a ship going to Tarshish: so he paid the fare thereof, and went down into it, to go with them unto Tarshish from the presence of the Lord" (Jonah 1:3).

The Ninevites were enemies of Israel, and Jonah didn't want to warn them of coming judgment, only to have them repent and be offered another chance because of God's gracious nature. He balked at the assignment God gave him, choosing instead to take a ship going in the opposite direction, to run as far away as possible. He stopped listening to God's voice. But God didn't let Jonah off the hook that easily.

God's Mercy on Full Display

A fierce storm came out of nowhere, causing the hearts of the seasoned sailors to melt. Awakened by the terrified men, Jonah recognized he was the reason for the foul weather and told the men to throw him overboard. The raging sea immediately became calm. Instead of drowning, Jonah's adventure continued when the Lord sent a giant fish to swallow him.

In the belly of the whale, Jonah prayed. Miraculously, God had the sea creature expel him onto dry land, giving Jonah a second chance. God's instructions to his prophet remained the same: "Arise, go unto Nineveh, that great city, and preach unto it the preaching that I bid thee" (Jonah 3:2).

Still hesitant, Jonah grudgingly preached to the Ninevites. The result was exactly what he had dreaded: the people repented, and God spared them. Now Jonah was furious. These barbaric enemies deserved punishment; instead, they received grace.

Jonah voiced his anger and despair to God: "Therefore now, O Lord, take, I beseech thee, my life from me; for it is better for me to die than to live" (Jonah 4:3). Because God didn't handle the situation the way Jonah wanted, he wished to die. But, instead of engaging in the conversation, God asked him a question, "...Doest thou well to be angry?" (Jonah 4:4b).

Like a petulant child, Jonah headed out of town without responding. He built a shelter in a location that allowed him to keep an eye on Nineveh. Maybe, just maybe, God would bring the judgment the people so clearly deserved.

God's Kindness Revealed

The Lord, in His kindness, allowed a plant to grow the next day, providing shade for Jonah in the sweltering heat. Jonah was thankful for the respite, but it was short-lived. The next morning, the plant was dead. As the wind blew and the sun beat down on Jonah, he felt faint and once again wanted to die.

The Lord continued to pursue Jonah despite his anger and stubborn refusal to listen. Again, God questioned Jonah. Was he justified in being angry? Jonah clung defiantly to his poor attitude: "...I do well to be angry, even unto death" (Jonah 4:9b).

God's answer stopped him in his tracks. Jonah had pitied the plant that died, despite having done nothing to plant it or cause it to grow. God's next words revealed His heart, "And should not I spare Nineveh, that great city, wherein are more than sixscore thousand persons that cannot discern between their right hand and their left hand...?" (Jonah 4:11).

Even when Jonah actively ran from God, drowning out His words, the Lord mercifully pursued him, giving him more opportunities to obey Him. I'm so thankful the same was true in my darkest days. Though I gave up on reading His Word, He never abandoned His pursuit of me. And He won't give up on you.

God's Character

Reading the book of Jonah and the other books of the Bible gives us a rich understanding of who God is. From Genesis to Revelation, He reveals Himself clearly to us. Scripture describes Him as:

- **Omnipotent** (All-Powerful)
- **Omniscient** (All-Knowing)
- **Holy** (Pure and Righteous)
- **Loving** (Full of Love)

- **Just** (Fair and Impartial)
- **Merciful** (Compassionate and Forgiving)
- **Faithful** (Reliable and Trustworthy)

A full list of Scriptures corresponding to each characteristic is included in Appendix C.

He is all of these things and infinitely more.

Our Identity in Christ

God desires a close relationship with us. When we are His adopted children, we have a brand-new identity. These are just a few of the characteristics that describe us:

- **Blessed**
- **Chosen**
- **Adopted**
- **Redeemed and forgiven**
- **Sealed with the Holy Spirit**
- **Holy**
- **Victorious**

For Scripture references that support each of these truths, see Appendix D.

This is who we are. As we read God's Word, we gain a clearer understanding of His nature and His great love for us. Our relationship with Him deepens, and our faith grows stronger. When we truly understand our identity in Christ, we are set free from the grip of false guilt and shame. Let His Word be your guide and source of comfort. Embrace your identity as His beloved child.

 Your Turn: Reflection Questions and Action Steps

Pause and Reflect

1. Have symptoms of anxiety or depression affected your Bible reading and time with the Lord?

2. How has your understanding of God's character shaped the way you navigate anxiety and depression?

3. How have feelings of worthlessness or spiritual struggle affected your perception of God's love and care?

4. How do you distinguish between guilt and shame in your own experience? In what ways has this understanding impacted your spiritual and emotional growth?

5. How do you respond when God doesn't act the way you expect Him to? Ask Him to search your heart for hidden bitterness or resentment. If He reveals something, confess it and move forward, confident of God's forgiveness and love.

6. What truths about God's character stood out to you in Jonah's story? How might those same truths apply to your current struggles?

7. How does recognizing your new identity in Christ, as blessed, chosen, and adopted, shape the way you view yourself and your relationship with Him?

Live It Out

1. **Establish a morning routine:** Choose a Bible reading plan and start with just a few verses a day. If you struggle to focus, try an audio version.

2. **Challenge spiritual doubts:** Revisit the gospel regularly. Write down key Scriptures that affirm your salvation and God's unchanging love.

3. **Reflect on God's character:** Meditate on His attributes: mercy, grace, justice, holiness, and faithfulness. Choose one to focus on each day and look for ways He displays it in your life.

4. **Address feelings of worthlessness with truth:** Remind yourself daily of God's unconditional love. Keep a list of verses that highlight His care for you and refer to them often.

5. **Discern the difference between guilt and shame:** Guilt points to specific actions. Confess them to God and receive His forgiveness (1 John 1:9). Shame attacks your identity; when it surfaces, replace the lies with affirming truths of who you are in Christ.

6. **Reach out for support:** Confide in a trusted friend about your struggles with anxiety, depression, or spiritual doubts. Be honest about any guilt or shame you're carrying and allow your friend to walk alongside you with prayer and encouragement.

7. **Embrace your identity in Christ:** Write out Scripture-based affirmations that remind you who you are in Him. Take one step to live in light of that truth today, whether by walking in holiness, serving someone else, or relying on the Holy Spirit's strength.

Can I Pray for You?

Heavenly Father, Thank You for the gift of Your Word. It is Your love letter to us, teaching, correcting, and instructing us in how to live for You. It is living, active, and powerful— sharper than any sword. It penetrates the depths of our minds, discerning both our thoughts and the intentions behind them. Anxiety and depression can cloud our minds, making it difficult to concentrate, focus on the truth, or feel motivated to read the Bible. Fill us with the desire to spend time with You. Help us have an accurate view of who You are. You are sovereign, holy, just, all-powerful, all-knowing, present everywhere, unchanging, loving, merciful, kind, and faithful. Let this knowledge encourage us to confess any sin to You, knowing You are ready and willing to shower us with forgiveness. Put Your finger on any false guilt we're holding onto and give us grace to release it. Protect us from the shame that creeps in, accusing us that we are unworthy of Your love. This is not of You, and we renounce it in the name of Jesus. Replace self-condemnation with an accurate view of our identity in Christ. Your Word is clear: we are blessed, chosen, adopted, accepted, redeemed, forgiven, righteous, beloved by You, and sealed with the Holy Spirit. Because of the work You've done in our lives, we pursue holiness. You declare we are more than conquerors in Christ. We embrace our identity in You. We choose to trust You today. In Jesus' mighty name, Amen.

Works Cited

[1] Cartreine, James. "More than Sad: Depression Affects Your Ability to Think." *Harvard Health Blog*, 6 May 2016, https://www.health.harvard.edu/blog/sad-depression-affects-ability-think-201605069551. Accessed 14 July 2025.

[2] Cartreine, James. "More than Sad: Depression Affects Your Ability to Think." *Harvard Health Blog*, 6 May 2016, https://www.health.harvard.edu/blog/sad-depression-affects-ability-think-201605069551. Accessed 14 July 2025.

[3] National Institute of Mental Health. "Depression." *National Institute of Mental Health*, 2024, https://www.nimh.nih.gov/health/publications/depression. Accessed 15 July 2025.

[4] Leahy, Robert L. "How to Build Motivation to Overcome Depression." *Psychology Today*, 19 Apr. 2021, https://www.psychologytoday.com/us/blog/anxiety-files/202104/how-build-motivation-overcome-depression. Accessed 15 July 2025.

[5] Vallance, David. "Depression, Anxiety and the Christian." *Web Truth*, 4 Oct. 2024, https://www.webtruth.org/cultural-issues/depression-anxiety-and-the-christian/. Accessed 15 July 2025.

[6] Pederson, Traci. "Understanding Spiritual Depression." *Psych Central*, 29 Jan. 2024, https://psychcentral.com/depression/spiritual-depression. Accessed 15 July 2025.

[7] Staff Reports. "Shame, Guilt, and the Wesley Brothers." *The Times Gazette*, 29 Jan. 2025, https://www.timesgazette.com/2025/01/29/shame-guilt-and-the-wesley-brothers/. Accessed 15 July 2025.

[8] Staff Reports. "Shame, Guilt, and the Wesley Brothers." *The Times Gazette*, 29 Jan. 2025, https://www.timesgazette.com/2025/01/29/shame-guilt-and-the-wesley-brothers/. Accessed 15 July 2025.

[9] Staff Reports. "Shame, Guilt, and the Wesley Brothers." *The Times Gazette*, 29 Jan. 2025, https://www.timesgazette.com/2025/01/29/shame-guilt-and-the-wesley-brothers/. Accessed 15 July 2025.

7

Talk to the One Who Made You

My Life Lesson

In all honesty, it's easier for me to read and study the Bible than to still my thoughts and talk to God in prayer. Much like giving a polite, surface-level answer when someone asks how I'm doing, I often do the same with the Lord—sharing what's easy rather than what's deep and difficult. Vulnerability isn't easy, especially when you've believed the lie that you have to measure up to be accepted.

Maybe you've felt that way, too. Whether it's the discomfort of uncovering what's been carefully hidden or the distraction of a restless mind and a long to-do list, prayer can feel challenging. But the truth is, we *need* to communicate with our Heavenly Father every day. He invites us to come. He can handle everything we bring to Him. These realities fill us with hope and stir eager anticipation to meet with Him.

As anxiety took hold in 2021, I don't remember making a deliberate decision to stop praying, but I do recall slipping into a place of fear. I wasn't confident I'd make it through another intense mental battle. *Was God disappointed in me?* I felt so alone. Anxious thoughts looped endlessly, crowding out every opportunity to pray.

Overwhelmed by a pervasive sense of dread, my faith in God began to waver. Instead of recognizing my emotions as valuable tools that alerted me to something needing to be addressed at the soul level, I let them take control.

When I talked to the Lord, it felt more like I was just going through the motions. My prayers sounded rehearsed, repeating the same hollow words again and again. At night, when I couldn't sleep, I would pray verses from the Bible, hoping I would drift off. But when sleep didn't come, I found myself worrying about how the lack of rest would impact me the next day. My heart would race, my muscles would tighten, and my breathing would become shallow.

Anger and Suppressed Emotions

The longer the anxiety and depression dragged on, the harder it became to talk to the Lord. The sense of punishment lingered, and with it came anger. I didn't like the Lord's silence. Although I knew God was aware of my thoughts, I didn't want to acknowledge the inner turmoil that lay just below the surface.

Only after my healing did my husband and I discover the root of that anger. It stemmed from not having a voice as a child. The conflict I witnessed at home caused me to shut down, and the instructions to keep family matters within the family silenced me further.

As a result, I learned to suppress my emotions and pretend everything was fine, even when it wasn't. I became the good girl who followed the rules, aimed for perfection, and tried to earn the approval of others. Somewhere along the way, I began to equate being accepted with being flawless. Mistakes felt dangerous. Every slip-up seemed to bring me one step closer to my deepest fear—rejection.

I carried that mindset into adulthood. Even after coming to know Christ, I found it difficult to rest fully in His love. Grace was hard to receive. Deep down, I still felt like I had to measure up to an unwritten standard to secure His acceptance. I believed God's Word when it said He loved me, but I lived as though His love was conditional. My actions revealed the truth: there were heart-level issues I hadn't yet uncovered or surrendered.

Questioning My Worth

Anxiety and depression became the catalysts that forced me to explore the deeper places of my heart. For years, I had operated under the weight of perfectionism. Anytime I failed to meet my unrealistic expectations, I was flooded with false guilt. But when I truly sinned, choosing my own way over God's, I felt the sting of real guilt. I asked for forgiveness, but over time, the two types of guilt merged, forming a deep-rooted belief that something was inherently wrong with *me*.

I didn't realize how harshly I viewed myself until everything fell apart. All those years of striving, people-pleasing, and trying to keep it all together came crashing in like a wave, and I was swallowed by the lie that I didn't measure up, and never would. After my suicide attempts,

I couldn't escape the pit of shame I had created. I hated myself for what I had done. Feeling like a complete failure as a wife, a mother, and a believer, the voices in my head accused me daily: *God could never forgive you. You're worthless. You'll never be free.*

A feeling of hopelessness settled in. I didn't believe anyone could help me. I couldn't admit my horrific actions to myself. *How could I talk to a holy God about them?* God was still good, but I didn't think He wanted anything to do with me. *Why would He?* I had utterly failed. The image I carried of God during that time was of someone far off, displeased with me, and determined to make me pay for what I'd done.

Rumination became my constant companion. Before my suicide attempts, I was consumed with identifying the cause of my anxiety and depression. Some days I blamed the sin of comparison; other days I pointed to my diet or hormones. It wasn't uncommon to come up with more than a dozen possible causes in a single day.

After the attempts, my thoughts grew darker. I became overwhelmed by the fear of eternal separation from God. I knew what Scripture said about grace, but I didn't believe it applied to me—not anymore.

Falling for the Lie

I began taking numerous Bible verses out of context. My thoughts swung between believing I had hardened my heart like Pharaoh (beyond forgiveness) and pleading with God for mercy. In one of the few journal entries I wrote in 2023, I noted these verses in Ephesians:

Be ye therefore followers of God, as dear children; And walk in love, as Christ also hath loved us, and hath given himself for us an offering and a sacrifice to God for a sweetsmelling savour. But fornication, and all uncleanness, or covetousness, let it not be once named among you, as becometh saints; Neither filthiness, nor foolish talking, nor jesting, which are not convenient: but rather giving of thanks. For this ye know, that no whoremonger, nor unclean person, nor covetous man, who is an idolater, hath any inheritance in the kingdom of Christ and of God.

—Ephesians 5:1–5

I responded with the following prayer:

Lord, I have not been walking in love. I can identify with the sins listed in verses three and four, especially foolish talking. I've not been giving thanks. I am a miserable sinner...I don't want to have an evil heart of unbelief. Help me know the truth about my salvation.

Ashamed of what I'd done and unable to sense God's forgiveness, I believed the accuser's lie: the sin of attempting suicide was too big for God to pardon. Guilt and shame gripped my heart. The more I avoided talking to the Lord, the tighter the grip became.

When I couldn't pray, others stood in the gap for me, my husband, family, and friends. Their faithful prayers slowly reintroduced me to the truth of who God is. Over time, that truth led me back to His throne of grace.

The Science Behind It

We are complex individuals navigating lives full of challenging situations. What influences our decision to open up about our struggles in some moments and remain silent in others?

We often speak out when we're longing for support. When family, friends, or professionals offer emotional strength and understanding, we no longer carry our burdens alone. Relationships are strengthened when we trust others and connect on a deeper, more meaningful level.

Verbalizing difficult experiences helps us address, process, and work through what we're feeling. Having the freedom to discuss challenging topics can also lead to helpful advice, fresh perspectives, and practical solutions.[1]

If you look closely, the common thread behind our willingness to be vulnerable is a longing for connection. But if connection is what we long for, why do we sometimes pull away instead?

When I was wrestling with anxiety, depression, and the aftermath of my suicide attempts, shame silenced me. I didn't want anyone to see the overwhelming mess I felt inside. Everything had to remain hidden, carefully tucked away. I kept quiet for many of the following reasons:

- **Fear of judgment:** Worrying about being judged, misunderstood, or rejected can keep us from opening up.[2]
- **Emotional overwhelm:** Some problems feel too painful or overwhelming to talk about. Avoiding them can seem like the only way to prevent reliving

trauma or facing emotions we don't know how to express.[3]

- **Perceived futility:** Believing that sharing our struggle won't change the situation or solve the problem can make conversations feel distressing and pointless.[4]

- **Protective mechanism:** Sometimes, staying silent feels like a way to protect ourselves from further emotional pain. It can shield us from vulnerability and help us maintain a sense of control.[5]

Each of these reasons is rooted in an inward focus driven by fear. Anxiety and depression further complicate matters, affecting both the desire to communicate and the ability to do so effectively. Both conditions are marked by rumination: the tendency to dwell on the same dark thoughts, repeatedly revisiting causes, consequences, and symptoms of distress.[6] This internal struggle doesn't just affect what we say; it impacts whether we speak at all.

When Words Don't Come Easily

Anxiety often leads to overthinking.[7] The fear of saying the wrong thing makes it difficult to express ourselves freely. To avoid feelings of nervousness or panic, we may steer clear of interactions altogether. Difficulty concentrating can also lead to unclear communication.

I experienced all of this firsthand. I'll never forget the painfully silent eight-hour car ride with my husband. I spoke fewer than a dozen words the entire time. An irrational fear that I might say something that would upset him plagued me, and I elected to stay quiet.

Depression has its own set of struggles. A lack of motivation can make it extremely difficult to communicate effectively. Feelings of worthlessness make it difficult to share and can lead to self-imposed isolation.[8] Fatigue can further drain the energy needed for meaningful conversations. A pessimistic mindset can also influence discussions, shifting our focus to the negative rather than the hopeful.

Both anxiety and depression can trap us in a cycle where ineffective communication deepens our isolation. Isolation, in turn, intensifies their symptoms. This same pattern, avoiding conversation out of fear or pain, often carries over into our relationship with God.

How Emotions Can Affect Prayer

When powerful emotions, especially anger, go unexpressed, they can block our ability to pray honestly. Sometimes we feel hurt and disappointed, convinced God hasn't heard us. At other times, our pride prevents us from admitting we're struggling. When we fear the Lord may reject or judge us for our anger or doubts, it becomes difficult to be truthful with Him. Shame, guilt, and the desire to stay in control can all hold us back.

Whatever the reason, suppressed emotions can silence our prayers. But silence isn't always caused by defiance; it's often rooted in pain. That's why it's important to look more closely at what's behind the silence.

Here are several underlying factors that can keep us from connecting with God:

- **Emotional overload**: Suppressing emotions can cause them to build up over time. When they surface, the flood of feelings may be overwhelming, making it difficult to approach God in prayer.[9]

- **Fear of vulnerability**: Talking to God requires honesty and openness. If we've suppressed our emotions, we may be afraid to express our true feelings, even to Him.

- **Misunderstanding of God's nature**: We might have a distorted view of God, believing He doesn't want to hear about our struggles or that He will be disappointed in us. This misunderstanding can prevent us from seeking His comfort and guidance.

- **Past trauma**: Painful experiences, especially unresolved conflict or trauma, can cause us to suppress emotions. Old wounds may make it difficult to believe He is safe or trustworthy.

- **Lack of emotional awareness**: Sometimes we've buried our emotions so deeply that we're unaware of them. Without awareness, we don't know how to express our hearts in prayer.[10]

Have you been avoiding honest conversations with your Heavenly Father? Recognize the dangers of self-isolation and silence. Unaddressed emotions can take a serious toll on your physical, mental, and spiritual well-being.

But you don't have to stay stuck. When you recognize what's holding you back, you can bring it before your Creator and begin praying authentically once again.

Help and Hope from God's Word

The Bible is full of examples of God's people crying out to Him in prayer. Some of my favorite illustrations were penned by David.

The Lord inspired and preserved numerous psalms and passages of Scripture, giving us a front-row seat to David's life. His journey from shepherd boy to king was marked with both triumph and deep trial, including a season when Saul's jealousy drove him into hiding. During his years on the run and beyond, David wrote several psalms of lament. These were deeply personal songs that expressed anguish, repentance, and heartfelt pleas for God's intervention in some of his darkest moments.

Instead of burying his emotions, David recognized the need to share his burden with the Lord. Psalm 57 is a beautiful example of how he poured out his heart to the Lord without restraint:

> Be merciful unto me, O God, be merciful unto me: for my soul trusteth in thee: yea, in the shadow of thy wings will I make my refuge, until these calamities be overpast.

> I will cry unto God most high; unto God that performeth all things for me.

> He shall send from heaven, and save me from the reproach of him that would swallow me up. Selah. God shall send forth his mercy and his truth.

> My soul is among lions: and I lie even among them that are set on fire, even the sons of men, whose teeth are spears and arrows, and their tongue a sharp sword. Be

thou exalted, O God, above the heavens; let thy glory be above all the earth. They have prepared a net for my steps; my soul is bowed down: they have digged a pit before me, into the midst whereof they are fallen themselves. Selah.

My heart is fixed, O God, my heart is fixed: I will sing and give praise.

Awake up, my glory; awake, psaltery and harp: I myself will awake early.

I will praise thee, O Lord, among the people: I will sing unto thee among the nations.

For thy mercy is great unto the heavens, and thy truth unto the clouds.

Be thou exalted, O God, above the heavens: let thy glory be above all the earth.

—Psalm 57

David didn't hold back. He begged for mercy, asked for rescue, and praised God for deliverance, even before his circumstances changed.

When our burdens threaten to crush us, we can adopt David's attitude, one of trust and openness, knowing that our God is trustworthy and always attentive to the cries of our hearts.

David's Honesty

When King Saul continued pursuing him, David took his unfiltered laments to God:

Deliver me from mine enemies, O my God: defend me from them that rise up against me.

Deliver me from the workers of iniquity, and save me from bloody men.

For, lo, they lie in wait for my soul: the mighty are gathered against me; not for my transgression, nor for my sin, O Lord.

They run and prepare themselves without my fault: awake to help me, and behold.

—Psalm 59:1–4

David affirmed his innocence, insisting he did not deserve to be hunted down. In an act of raw honesty, he even begs God to "wake up," as though He were sleeping, since deliverance hadn't come yet.

David didn't shy away from sharing his deepest struggles with God because he knew God could handle even the most painful emotions. David's trust didn't depend on his feelings; it rested on God's character.

Like David, we may feel hunted—not by a king, but by our thoughts, fears, or past. And like David, we have a choice: stay silent or pour it all out before the Lord.

A Season of Silence

David shared a deeply authentic relationship with the Lord. Yet even David, the man God described as "a man after mine own heart" (1 Samuel 13:14), experienced a season when he avoided talking to his heavenly Father. You probably remember the story.

After committing adultery with Bathsheba and orchestrating the murder of her husband, Uriah, David entered a season of silence before God. For a time, it seemed

David's sin had gone undetected. But God knew. He sent the prophet Nathan to confront David. Through a parable about a ewe lamb, the Lord exposed David's sin. Deeply convicted, David confessed his sin and pleaded for God's forgiveness.

David likely wrote Psalm 32 after his sin with Bathsheba and the subsequent confrontation with Nathan. It clearly describes the distress David felt when he remained silent and the relief he found when he confessed:

> Blessed is he whose transgression is forgiven, whose sin is covered.

> Blessed is the man unto whom the Lord imputeth not iniquity, and in whose spirit there is no guile.

> When I kept silence, my bones waxed old through my roaring all the day long.

> For day and night thy hand was heavy upon me: my moisture is turned into the drought of summer. Selah.

> I acknowledged my sin unto thee, and mine iniquity have I not hid. I said, I will confess my transgressions unto the Lord; and thou forgavest the iniquity of my sin. Selah.

> —Psalm 32:1–5

Emotional and Physical Distress

Did you notice David's description of keeping silent? His groaning aged his bones, and he felt the excruciating physical and psychological effects of carrying unconfessed sin. It is important to note that experiencing anxiety and depression are not indicators of sin. The key to remember is the Lord's response when David repented and began speaking to Him again. God forgave him completely, and their relationship was restored.

A striking contrast emerges between the moments David poured out his heart to the Lord and the times he remained silent. Drawing from another Psalm David wrote during this period in his life, we see a glimpse of God's desire for each of us: "Behold, thou desirest truth in the inward parts: and in the hidden part thou shalt make me to know wisdom" (Psalm 51:6).

David's full trust in God led to open, honest communication. God longs for us to come to Him with everything, keeping no secrets and willingly addressing what He points out. The result? Our hearts will be transformed and will be filled with His truth and wisdom.

 Your Turn: Reflection Questions and Action Steps

Pause and Reflect

1. What are some reasons you might avoid talking about your struggle with anxiety and depression?

2. How do you view the role of emotions in your spiritual life? Do you see them as indicators of areas that need attention or healing?

3. How does your understanding of God's nature affect your willingness to be open and honest in prayer?

4. Reflect on past experiences of conflict or trauma. How have they shaped your ability to trust God and communicate with others?

5. How do you typically respond to guilt and shame? What helps you seek forgiveness and move forward?

6. In what ways do you express your emotions to God? Are there specific Psalms or prayers that resonate with you?

7. How might identifying the root causes of your hesitation to pray help deepen your relationship with God?

Live It Out

1. **Educate yourself on anxiety and depression:** Learn how these conditions impact communication and develop a strategy to manage them.

2. **Address unresolved emotions:** Identify any past wounds or lingering emotions that may be interfering with your connection to God. Consider biblical counseling or joining a support group to begin your healing journey.

3. **Meditate on God's nature:** Reflect on His love, grace, and patience. Let these truths reshape your perspective on prayer and encourage open, heartfelt communication.

4. **Create space for prayer:** Set aside a specific time each day to communicate with God, even when it feels uncomfortable at first. Find a private place where you can quiet your thoughts and focus on talking to Him.

5. **Be honest with God:** Like David, pour out your heart to Him. Bring your anger, fear, sadness, or

doubt (whatever it is) without holding back. He can handle it.

6. **Study psalms of lament:** Read passages like Psalms 32, 57, and 59. Pay attention to the emotions David expressed and how he cried out to the Lord.

7. **Find a prayer partner:** Invite a trusted friend, family member, or mentor to support you in prayer. Share your goals and commit to checking in regularly. Praying together can build connection and courage.

Can I Pray for You?

Heavenly Father, Thank You for the gift of prayer and communication. Thank You for knowing and understanding us better than we know ourselves. Your Word is clear: You are acquainted with all our ways. You know the words we speak and the very thoughts we think, and You love us beyond what we can imagine. You're not surprised by our anxious thoughts or our downcast souls. You invite us to be honest with You. We see numerous examples in David's life where he did not hesitate to express everything he felt: his doubts, concerns, and even his anger. You didn't turn him away. You listened and provided comfort. Help us be transparent in prayer, trusting that You will hear and answer according to Your will and in Your perfect timing. Assure us of Your presence. Forgive us when we don't fully trust You. Help us meditate on who You are. Give us the grace to confront any unresolved emotions or traumas in our lives, knowing that by bringing them into the light, we will draw closer to You and invite healing. Lord, You desire our innermost being to be filled with truth and wisdom. Thank You for putting us in families and communities. Give us the strength to reach out and ask a friend to join us in prayer today. In Jesus' name, Amen.

Works Cited

[1] Buckingham, Louise. "The Power of Community: Why Sharing Problems Brings Healing." *The AOC*, 6 Dec. 2024, https://www.theaoc.org.uk/the-power-of-community-why-sharing-problems-brings-healing/. Accessed 25 July 2025.

[2] "How Can I Overcome the Fear of Being Judged by Others According to Biblical Teachings?" *CrossTalk*, 12 July 2024, https://biblechat.ai/knowledgebase/wellbeing/emotional-health/how-can-i-overcome-fear-being-judged-others-according-biblical-teachings/. Accessed 25 July 2025.

[3] Parke, Blair. "Is It Okay to Feel Overwhelmed as a Christian?" *Bible Study Tools*, Salem Web Network, 22 June 2022, https://www.biblestudytools.com/bible-study/topical-studies/is-it-okay-to-feel-overwhelmed-as-a-christian.html. Accessed 25 July 2025.

[4] Mayo Clinic. "Mental Health: Overcoming the Stigma of Mental Illness." *Mayo Clinic*, Mayo Foundation for Medical Education and Research, 24 May 2017, https://www.mayoclinic.org/diseases-conditions/mental-illness/in-depth/mental-health/art-20046477. Accessed 29 July 2025.

[5] Lindberg, Sara. "What Is Emotional Numbness? Can We Really Be 'Comfortably Numb'?" *Verywell Mind*, Dotdash Meredith, 20 Mar. 2025, https://www.verywellmind.com/emotional-numbing-symptoms-2797372. Accessed 29 July 2025.

[6] Nolen-Hoeksema, Susan, et al. "Rethinking Rumination." *Perspectives on Psychological Science*, vol. 3, no. 5, 2008, pp. 400-24. https://pubmed.ncbi.nlm.nih.gov/26158958/. Accessed 25 July 2025.

[7] Morin, Amy. "How to Stop Overthinking: Here's How to Recognize the Signs That You're Overthinking." *Verywell Mind*, Dotdash Meredith, 18 June 2024, https://www.verywellmind.com/how-to-know-when-youre-overthinking-5077069. Accessed 25 July 2025.

[8] Robb-Dover, Kristina. "Breaking the Cycle of Self-Isolating and Depression - An Interview with Dr. Michael Jochananov." *FHE Health - Addiction & Mental Health Care*, 21 May 2020, https://fherehab.com/learning/self-isolating-depression-with-dr-j/. Accessed 25 July 2025.

[9] NAMI. "Critical Things to Know about Emotions for Mental Health and Healing." *NAMI*, 23 Jan. 2023, https://www.nami.org/anxiety-disorders/critical-things-to-know-about-emotions-for-mental-health-and-healing/. Accessed 25 July 2025.

[10] NAMI. "Critical Things to Know about Emotions for Mental Health and Healing." *NAMI*, 23 Jan. 2023, https://www.nami.org/anxiety-disorders/critical-things-to-know-about-emotions-for-mental-health-and-healing/. Accessed 25 July 2025.

8

Worship Through the Storm

My Life Lesson

Each morning as I get ready, I choose a playlist to uplift and encourage me. The music is turned up loud enough to rise above the running water and the drone of the hairdryer. I gravitate toward songs that remind me of God's character, His love, mercy, and unfailing hope. Those melodies play over in my mind the rest of the day.

I can't point to the exact date when it changed, but as anxiety and depression increased, my listening to Scripture-saturated songs decreased.

Over the years, Steve and I have had the joy of working with young people in the music ministry. That ministry grew and evolved, eventually leading him to set up a recording studio in our home. With his rare gift, an ear finely tuned to detail and a passion for recording, mixing, and mastering, he began producing music under his label, Go Ye Records. Today, those songs have been played nearly half a million times, touching hearts in more than fifty countries around the world.

Ironically, as we were witnessing the impact of music on others, I found myself withdrawing from it. My desire to listen to music or lift my voice in praise gradually faded. My focus shifted away from the One who offered strength in my struggles and toward the troubling question: *Why is this happening to me?* Unable to make sense of it, I allowed anger and discouragement to take root in my soul.

Silence Instead of Song

Instead of listening to music throughout the day, I craved silence. Truth-filled lyrics stirred up feelings of guilt and condemnation. They were the same emotions I battled when trying to read God's Word. The longer I distanced myself from connecting with God through worship, the more vulnerable I became to the enemy's attacks. Dark thought patterns took root, and gratitude was gradually replaced by complaints.

When Steve traveled for business, the hours of the day seemed to stretch endlessly, but the evenings were the hardest. As twilight gave way to complete darkness, my anxiety intensified. The silence I welcomed during the day became oppressive at night, and I felt compelled to turn on the radio. Shame clung to me like a heavy garment, making it hard to embrace the lyrics. More often than not, I'd reach my limit and turn it off again.

A Source of Help and Hope

For Steve, music remained a place of solace. Throughout my battle with anxiety and depression, he turned to songs that expressed raw emotion and highlighted the Lord's power to meet people in their moments of need. Being my caregiver was emotionally draining, and at times, he would watch a particular music video, along with its story, again and again for encouragement. In that season, music became a source of help and hope for him.

Despite the challenges, Steve had the opportunity to organize, produce, and present two concerts during my illness. Both events required hours of practice, yet he remained dedicated to maintaining a sense of normalcy in our home. As I was distancing myself from friends, he was inviting musicians over to our house for practice sessions.

By then, Steve had taken over most of the household chores, and I didn't have the energy, or the desire, to help. The idea of people coming into our home for music rehearsals filled me with dread. I'd force a quick hello, then disappear into our bedroom, hoping no one would notice. Engaging in small talk when it felt like my world was imploding was too much to handle.

I imagined all the critical things they must be thinking: *What's wrong with her? She looks so tired. Why doesn't she talk more?* Every time laughter echoed from the studio, it shook me. I was certain I was the quiet target of their amusement, someone they didn't know how to talk to and couldn't begin to help. The more I isolated myself, the louder the negative thoughts reverberated.

It wasn't just the noise; it was the reminder that life was moving on without me, and I felt powerless to stop it. In all honesty, I was jealous of the time Steve spent on music, despite having no interest in it myself. My desperate need to hold on kept me in self-protection mode, while intrusive thoughts whispered: *You're going to lose him.*

Even as disjointed thoughts swirled through my mind, I couldn't fully escape the music. It drifted through the walls, notes and lyrics, colliding with the shame I carried. A part of me longed to believe the words were true. But the lies screamed louder: *You've gone too far. You're beyond help. You can't turn back.*

When the last guests left and the door finally closed, I felt a moment of relief—only to be swallowed by a deeper emptiness. I was miserable.

Missed Opportunities

When the day of the first concert arrived, I didn't attend. The thought of arriving hours early, forcing myself to make conversation, and watching my husband set up equipment and run through last-minute rehearsals made me sick. I stayed home and crawled into bed, hoping sleep would drown out the relentless soundtrack of guilt in my mind. Instead, I lay awake for hours, my heightened senses analyzing every sound: the eerie call of a screech owl, a scritch-scratch that sent chills up my spine, and then the sudden boom of fireworks. *Fireworks? Why would there be a celebration this time of year?* Uninvited, the thoughts gripped me with panic. By staying away from the concert, I missed another chance to let songs of praise break into the darkness that surrounded me.

Eighteen months later, another concert was planned, this time a Good Friday event at our church. By then, I had been in psychosis for four months, and every week brought new challenges. With treatment options dwindling, Steve was urged to consider placing me in a residential facility. The weight of the situation was crushing. He considered canceling the concert but chose to move forward, trusting God to provide what was needed.

Just like before, I chose to stay home rather than attend the performance. I busied myself sterilizing our bathroom cabinets, intent on ridding the area of every single germ. It was easier to scrub drawers than face the chaos inside. Although my thoughts remained irrational and confused, I found myself drawn to the live-stream. The concert was beautiful. Tears streamed down my face as each song was sung. *Why am I reacting like this?*

A mix of guilt and gratitude washed over me as I thought about how much my husband had poured into the event. Guilt for not being supportive, yet grateful he had followed through with the event. My thoughts remained conflicted. Despite the strain in our relationship, I couldn't help feeling proud of my husband. At the time, it was impossible to see, but God was weaving purpose through all the pain.

Never Alone

During my two-and-a-half-year illness, several popular songs were released by Christian artists that addressed anxiety and depression. Even though I felt alone in my battle, it was a misconception. The enemy capitalized on that lie, tempting me to avoid the music that could have kept my heart tender and open to the truth. For a time, his ruse worked. But his craftiness was ultimately no match for God's power.

Looking back, I can see how the Holy Spirit was at work even when I resisted. At the time, I didn't enjoy listening to Christian music because it stirred a deep sense of guilt. I believed my suicide attempts had placed me beyond God's forgiveness. The songs I once loved became painful reminders of what I thought I had lost.

Beneath the guilt was anger: anger at the Lord for not rescuing me. And yet, despite my resistance, I couldn't completely shut the music out. The lyrics still rang true. They spoke of grace, mercy, and love: truths I couldn't feel but couldn't deny.

Although I didn't realize it at the time, the Holy Spirit was tenderly softening my heart, preparing me for the healing that would eventually come. What I once resisted became one of the very tools God used to rebuild my trust in Him.

The Science Behind It

My experience of avoiding music stands in sharp contrast to how God designed it to impact us. God created us to worship. While there are many ways to express that worship (through prayer, reading Scripture, fasting, giving, and serving), listening to Christ-centered music and singing songs of praise often top the list.

Strangely enough, when I was overcome with anxiety and depression, I couldn't bring myself to listen to music, much less sing. The false guilt and self-condemnation blocked the joy and connection I once felt when drawing near to God. Songs that once uplifted me now triggered pain, reminding me how far I thought I had fallen.

Yet music has long been a powerful tool for spiritual expression. The first song recorded in the Bible appears in the book of Exodus, celebrating the Israelites' deliverance from bondage in Egypt.

> Then sang Moses and the children of Israel this song unto the Lord, and spake, saying, I will sing unto the Lord, for he hath triumphed gloriously: the horse and his rider hath he thrown into the sea. The Lord is my strength and song, and he is become my salvation: he is my God, and I will prepare him an habitation; my father's God, and I will exalt him. The Lord is a man of war: the Lord is his name. Pharaoh's chariots and his host hath he cast into the sea: his chosen captains also are drowned in the Red sea.
>
> —Exodus 15:1–4

The song continues for several more verses and is followed by a second song sung by Moses' sister, Miriam, as she joyfully echoes God's goodness with tambourines and dancing.

Music and Singing: Powerful Forms of Worship

In simple terms, music is an art form that uses sound as its medium. According to the dictionary, it is defined as "vocal, instrumental, or mechanical sounds having rhythm, melody, or harmony. The science or art of ordering tones or sound in succession, in combination, and in temporal relationships to produce a composition having unity and continuity."[1] It has the power to evoke emotions, share truths, and unite people.

Research and personal experience point to its wide-ranging benefits: physically, mentally, and spiritually. Here are just a few of the ways listening to worship music can help:

Body:

- **Reduces stress:** Sacred songs can lower cortisol levels, helping our bodies unwind and relax.[2]
- **Supports heart health:** Calming melodies may reduce blood pressure and heart rate.[3]
- **Promotes better sleep:** Soft, slow-tempo arrangements can help create a peaceful atmosphere that encourages deeper, more restful sleep.[4]

Soul:

- **Elevates mood:** Uplifting praise can boost endorphins and dopamine, enhancing our mood and emotional resilience.[5]
- **Eases emotional pain:** Music offers comfort and peace in times of distress, anxiety, or sadness.[6]

Spirit:

- **Invites reflection:** Quiet moments with Christ-centered music provide space to meditate on the words and truths being expressed.[7]
- **Deepens faith:** Lyrics rooted in Scripture can draw us closer to the Lord, reinforcing our faith and offering encouragement.[8]

There's no doubt music has a profound impact on us when we consider how our brains process and respond to it. Music is now recognized as a therapeutic tool in modern medicine.

A Valuable Tool

Music therapy gained popularity following World War I and World War II. Community musicians visited veterans' hospitals to play for soldiers suffering from physical and emotional trauma.[9] According to the American Music Therapy Association, "The patients' consistent, positive physical and emotional responses to music led physicians and nurses to request that hospital administrators hire musicians to facilitate recovery."[10]

Although I didn't participate in formal music therapy during my illness, I find it fascinating to see how God's gift of music is being used in medical settings to bring comfort and healing, and history itself points to its power. Thousands of years earlier, King Saul's servants recommended music as a form of treatment:

> And Saul's servants said unto him, Behold now, an evil spirit from God troubleth thee. Let our lord now command thy servants, which are before thee, to seek out a man, who is a cunning player on an harp: and it shall come to pass, when the evil spirit from God is upon thee, that he shall play with his hand, and thou shalt be well.
>
> —1 Samuel 16:15–16

The Positive Impact of Music

It's important to understand that King Saul had willfully disobeyed God and refused to repent. As a result, the Lord allowed an evil spirit to torment him. Though Saul's rebellion left him in deep distress, music brought relief: "And it came to pass, when the evil spirit from God was upon Saul, that David took an harp, and played with his hand: so Saul was refreshed, and was well, and the evil spirit departed from him" (1 Samuel 16:23).

If music could have such a profound impact on King Saul, even in rebellion, how much more help and hope can it bring to those who are actively seeking the Lord? Music that reflects the truth of God's Word has the power to comfort, strengthen, and encourage those who pursue Him with open hearts.

During my season of psychosis, I avoided music, missing out on its benefits. But after my healing, as I reaffirmed my trust in God, I experienced its power in a new and fresh way. Songs rooted in Scripture proved life-giving, ministering grace, and restoring hope to my thirsty spirit.

The Benefits of Singing

Singing goes one step beyond merely listening to music; it invites us to actively participate. Here are a few of the many benefits of lifting our voices in song:

Body

- **Enhances physical health:** Singing involves deep breathing, which improves lung function and oxygenates the blood.[11]
- **Boosts immune system:** Some studies show it may increase levels of immunoglobulin A, an antibody that helps fight infection.[12]

Soul

- **Fosters engagement:** Singing draws us in, spiritually and emotionally, making the experience more personal and powerful.[13]

- **Improves focus:** By concentrating on lyrics, attention is redirected away from anxious thoughts, leading to greater clarity.[14]
- **Enhances memory and learning:** Scripture-based songs reinforce truth and aid in memorization.[15]

Spirit

- **Expresses gratitude:** Focusing on God's blessings through song nurtures a heart of thankfulness.[16]
- **Deepens connection with God:** Worshiping through music helps us express love and reverence, drawing us closer to Him.[17]
- **Strengthens community:** Singing with others fosters unity and a sense of belonging within the church community, reminding us that we are not alone.[18]

Aren't these beautiful gifts? Both listening to music and singing can have a profound impact on body, soul, and spirit. They are powerful, God-given tools to ease anxiety and depression, well worth incorporating into your daily rhythm of worship.

Help and Hope from God's Word

Science affirms the power of music, but Scripture shows us its purpose from the very beginning. Throughout the Bible, we see music used beautifully, not only in moments of victory but also in the valley.

Early in the book of Genesis, we find the first mention of music. Jubal, a descendant of Cain, is described as "the father of all such as handle the harp and organ" (Genesis 4:21). Later, music is introduced in worship for the first time as Moses and the Israelites celebrate their deliverance at the Red Sea. Meaningful lyrics, paired with simple instrumentation, were offered in praise to the Lord.

Through the inspiration of the Holy Spirit, the shepherd boy David penned numerous psalms, songs of worship dedicated to God. By the time David ascended the throne, he had intentionally woven music into Israel's temple worship. He organized singers and musicians by God's command, reminding us that worship through music wasn't David's idea, it was God's design: "And he set the Levites in the house of the Lord with cymbals, with psalteries, and with harps, according to the commandment of David, and of Gad the king's seer, and Nathan the prophet: for so was the commandment of the Lord by his prophets" (2 Chronicles 29:25).

A Pattern of Praise

This pattern of music as worship continues throughout both the Old and New Testaments. Time and again, God's people lifted their voices in praise after witnessing His miraculous provision: Deborah and Barak (Judges 5), Hannah (1 Samuel 2:1–10), David (Psalms 3, 34, 57, 63, 142), and Mary, the mother of Jesus (Luke 1:46–55), to name a few.

It's easy to relate to that kind of praise, gratitude that naturally overflows after answered prayer. But what about when the breakthrough hasn't come? What does it look like to lift a song of worship in the middle of the storm, when everything feels uncertain and there's no sign of relief?

A powerful example comes from the missionary journey of Paul and Silas, recorded in the book of Acts.

While preaching the gospel near Philippi, they encountered Lydia, a businesswoman whose heart the Lord opened. She and her family believed the message and were immediately baptized. Overflowing with gratitude, Lydia invited Paul and Silas to stay in her home during their time in the city.

Opposition and a Prison Sentence

As is often the case in ministry, opposition soon arose. A demon-possessed slave girl began following them. She worked as a fortune-teller, earning a great deal of money for her masters. Day after day, she harassed Paul and Silas, shouting and disrupting their ministry. After enduring the commotion for days, Paul rebuked the spirit in the name of Jesus, and the demon left her. She was set free.

While the girl may have rejoiced in her deliverance, her owners were furious. Their source of income was gone. In a fit of rage, they seized Paul and Silas and dragged them before the city officials.

Accused of disturbing the peace, they were publicly beaten and thrown into prison. Can you imagine their shock? They had helped someone, yet they were treated like criminals.

The jailer, under strict orders to keep them secure, put them in the inner cell and fastened their feet in wooden stocks. Immobilized and bleeding, Paul and Silas faced humiliation and injustice. Yet even then, they made a remarkable choice: "And at midnight Paul and Silas prayed, and sang praises unto God: and the prisoners heard them" (Acts 16:25).

Midnight Worship

Instead of lashing out at their accusers or wallowing in self-pity, these men turned to God in prayer. But their response didn't stop there. They lifted their voices in song to their Creator. Their bodies were battered, yet their spirits were lifted as they worshipped the Lord. They offered a sacrifice of praise, loud enough for the jailer and the other prisoners to hear.

Uncertain of the outcome, they refused to lose hope. In the darkest hour, they focused their gaze upward. Sometime after midnight, the impossible happened: "And suddenly there was a great earthquake, so that the foundations of the prison were shaken: and immediately all the doors were opened, and every one's bands were loosed" (Acts 16:26).

The jailer, jolted awake, assumed the prisoners had escaped. Fearing execution, he drew his sword to take his own life. But Paul's loud cry punctuated the chaos, stopping him. No one had left.

Overwhelmed, the jailer fell trembling before Paul and Silas. Only one question escaped his lips: "Sirs, what must I do to be saved?" (Acts 16:30b). The answer was simple and life-changing: "Believe on the Lord Jesus Christ, and thou shalt be saved..." (Acts 16:31). Without hesitation, he believed.

That very night, the jailer welcomed Paul and Silas into his home. He washed their wounds and watched as his whole household accepted the gospel and followed in baptism. What began as a prison sentence ended in revival.

The Ripple Effect of Praise

Little did Paul and Silas know their midnight songs would echo into eternity. The one who once held the keys to the jail now held the key to freedom—the truth that set him free. And it didn't stop with him: his entire family believed.

That kind of worship, praising God before the answer comes, might sound impossible. But Paul and Silas show us that it's not only possible, it's powerful.

Anxiety and depression may try to silence our voices, as they did mine, but worship through song lifts them higher. Worship acknowledges the weight of our struggle even as it declares trust in the One who holds the power to deliver.

 ## Your Turn: Reflection Questions and Action Steps

Pause and Reflect

1. When has music uplifted and encouraged you during a difficult season?

2. Has silence helped or hindered your healing during times of anxiety or depression?

3. What benefits have you noticed when you actively participate in worship?

4. How might singing, rather than just listening, help shift your focus from fear to faith?

5. What does Paul and Silas's midnight praise teach you about the power of worship in impossible circumstances?

6. Where might God be calling you to lift a song of worship even while you're still waiting for deliverance?

7. How could your personal expression of worship be used by God to encourage someone else?

Live It Out

1. **Incorporate praise music into your day:** Set aside 10 minutes to listen to Christ-centered music during morning devotions, on your commute, or before bedtime.

2. **Use music for emotional support:** Choose one worship song and reflect on its lyrics to draw encouragement and hope.

3. **Build a battle-ready playlist:** Create a short list of uplifting worship music to play during anxious or discouraging moments.

4. **Lift your voice in praise:** Sing along with one worship song today, even if softly or alone, and notice how it shifts your thoughts and spirit.

5. **Praise Him in retrospect:** Reflect on a "midnight hour" in your life and write a few lines of praise, thanking God for His presence in that season.

6. **Anchor in the Word:** Read Acts 16:25–34 slowly, journaling one truth about God's character that encourages you to worship even when it's hard.

7. **Pass along the praise:** Share a worship song that has encouraged you with a friend, and invite them to join you in lifting their eyes to the Lord.

Can I Pray for You?

Heavenly Father, Thank You for Your creativity. Your gift of music helps us in so many ways, allowing us to express our emotions and bringing You honor and glory. What a blessing that we have the opportunity to praise and worship You through song. We confess there are times when anxious thoughts and feelings of hopelessness threaten to keep us silent. Yet, just as Paul and Silas sang at midnight, help us lift our voices to You even in the storm, when deliverance seems impossible. Give us eyes to focus on You and faith to trust that victory belongs to You. Teach us to use music to combat negative thought patterns and to cultivate gratitude. When we're discouraged, replace the spirit of heaviness with the garment of praise. Put a new song in our hearts, songs that bless Your name and boldly proclaim the gospel to those around us. Remind us of all the ways You've worked miraculously in the past, and strengthen us to serve You with joy in the present. Give us the desire to gather with other believers, lifting our voices together in worship. You are good. Your mercy is everlasting, and Your truth will endure to every generation. Fill our mouths with Your praise. In Jesus' name, Amen.

Works Cited

1   "Music." *Merriam-Webster.com Dictionary*, Merriam-Webster, https://www.merriam-webster.com/dictionary/music. Accessed 31 July 2025.

2   Stanborough, Rebecca Joy. "The Benefits of Listening to Music." *Healthline*, 1 Apr. 2020, https://www.healthline.com/health/benefits-of-music. Accessed 31 July 2025.

3   Harvard Health Publishing. "Tuning In: How Music May Affect Your Heart." *Harvard Health*, 30 Mar. 2021, https://www.health.harvard.edu/heart-health/tuning-in-how-music-may-affect-your-heart. Accessed 31 July 2025.

4   Newsom, Rob, and Anis Rehman. "Music and Sleep." *Sleep Foundation*, 8 Nov. 2023, https://www.sleepfoundation.org/noise-and-sleep/music. Accessed 31 July 2025.

5   Boothby, Suzanne. "Does Music Affect Your Mood?" *Healthline*, 13 Apr. 2017, https://www.healthline.com/health-news/mental-listening-to-music-lifts-or-reinforces-mood-051713. Accessed 31 July 2025.

6   Boothby, Suzanne. "Does Music Affect Your Mood?" *Healthline*, 13 Apr. 2017, https://www.healthline.com/health-news/mental-listening-to-music-lifts-or-reinforces-mood-051713. Accessed 31 July 2025.

7   "The Importance of Music in Worship." *Church.org*, 11 Sept. 2024, https://church.org/the-importance-of-music-in-worship/. Accessed 31 July 2025.

8   "The Importance of Music in Worship." *Church.org*, 11 Sept. 2024, https://church.org/the-importance-of-music-in-worship/. Accessed 31 July 2025.

9   American Music Therapy Association. "History of Music Therapy." *Musictherapy.org*, 2019, https://www.musictherapy.org/about/history/. Accessed 31 July 2025.

10   American Music Therapy Association. *Music Therapy and Military Populations: A Status Report and Recommendations on Music Therapy Treatment, Programs, Research, and Practice Policy.* 2014, https://www.musictherapy.org/assets/1/7/MusicTherapyMilitaryPops_2014.pdf. Accessed 1 August 2025.

11   Chamageri, Joan. "17 Incredible Benefits of Singing." *Healthier Steps*, 8 July 2023, https://healthiersteps.com/17-incredible-benefits-of-singing/. Accessed 1 August 2025.

12   Chamageri, Joan. "17 Incredible Benefits of Singing." *Healthier Steps*, 8 July 2023, https://healthiersteps.com/17-incredible-benefits-of-singing/. Accessed 1 August 2025.

13   R., Michael. "The Spiritual Power of Song: Importance of Singing in Worship." *SingingLessons.co*, 25 Oct. 2023, https://singinglessons.co/importance-of-singing-in-worship/. Accessed 1 Aug. 2025.

14   Hays, Kate F. "Twelve Reasons for Singing." *Psychology Today*, Dec. 2014, https://www.psychologytoday.com/us/blog/the-edge-peak-performance-psychology/201412/twelve-reasons-singing. Accessed 1 Aug. 2025.

15   R., Michael. "The Spiritual Power of Song: Importance of Singing in Worship." *SingingLessons.co*, 25 Oct. 2023, https://singinglessons.co/importance-of-singing-in-worship/. Accessed 1 Aug. 2025.

16   "Worship Songs about Gratitude." *Repeat Replay*, 12 Feb. 2024, https://repeatreplay.com/worship-songs-about-gratitude/. Accessed 1 Aug. 2025.

17   R., Michael. "The Spiritual Power of Song: Importance of Singing in Worship." *SingingLessons.co*, 25 Oct. 2023, https://singinglessons.co/importance-of-singing-in-worship/. Accessed 1 Aug. 2025.

18   R., Michael. "The Spiritual Power of Song: Importance of Singing in Worship." *SingingLessons.co*, 25 Oct. 2023, https://singinglessons.co/importance-of-singing-in-worship/. Accessed 1 Aug. 2025.

Part 4:

Keys to Overcoming the Enemy's Traps and Walking in Freedom

*In the earlier sections of this book, we've explored both the science and the Scripture behind anxiety and depression. Part 4 shifts the focus fully to the spiritual realm. Here, you'll discover God's battle-tested plan for overcoming the enemy's traps: practical, faith-filled steps to walk in lasting freedom.

9

Do the Internal Work

My Life Lesson

September 1, 2023, will forever be etched in my mind as a day of celebration. It was the day I opened my hands in complete surrender to the One who controls all things.

Attending our ladies' Bible study for the first time since my anxiety returned marked a turning point. I walked into the room with trepidation and found my assigned seat. God used a friend's candid admission about her struggle with negative thoughts and that day's lesson on redemption to break through the remaining chains that kept me bound. He invited me to step out of my prison cell with confident assurance.

Sitting in my Jeep in the church parking lot, I put into words what was buried deep in my heart: *"I trust You, Lord! I no longer want to live by these irrational beliefs. I want to be free."*

The moment I fully entrusted myself to my Heavenly Father, I immediately felt the fog of anxiety and depression lift. Just weeks before, I had been in the same parking lot, filled with fear, unable to bear the thought of staying at church one moment longer than necessary. But now, with sunlight streaming through my windshield, the weight I had carried for so long was gone.

Clarity displaced confusion. Peace replaced fear. Joy overcame the gloom. I could inhale deeply, finally able to rest. Instead of grasping for control, I realized God had been orchestrating everything all along, bringing healing in a way only He could.

Before the Breakthrough

Looking back, I can see how His hand was at work long before that day. In the months leading up to my breakthrough, I encountered daily reminders of His presence. One evening, when Steve took me out to eat, the waiter had just greeted us when I overheard the couple in the booth behind us talking about Jesus.

It seemed every errand exposed me to a conversation about the Lord. Each one filled me with guilt, reminding me how far I'd drifted from Him, but in His mercy, He was gently showing me He was near.

When anxiety was at its worst, I convinced myself I couldn't drive, yet there were times I had no choice. After my first suicide attempt, I entered an intensive outpatient program thirty minutes away that met three days a week. Gripping the steering wheel, fixing my eyes on the cars ahead, and doing everything I could to stay awake, I somehow made it safely to every session: further proof of God's grace.

During that season, my husband recommended a book that highlighted the role of a faithful, supportive wife. But after all I'd done, I feared I could never be that woman again. Yet, Steve was always willing to fight for me.

And the people I pushed away? They never stopped reaching out. All of these instances pointed to a Heavenly Father who cared deeply and never let me out of His sight.

Made Whole

That simple act of surrender marked an unmistakable shift in my relationship with the Lord. For too long, anxiety and depression had kept me bound, creating an emptiness that distanced me from His presence. But with healing came an overwhelming sense of His nearness. As tears of joy streamed down my face and my hands lifted in praise, I knew: only God could bring about such a renewal.

I shared the powerful transformation with my husband and a handful of close friends. For a few days, Steve and I kept the news to ourselves, letting the reality sink in. I was no longer tormented by the irrational thoughts that once consumed me. My mind was clear and calm. Peace flooded my soul. I knew God had healed me.

Steve sent a message to those who had faithfully walked alongside us throughout our battle:

Through years of prayer, and because of faithful family and friends like you, Maria is healed. Trust me, I know exactly how hard to believe that is. I kept it to myself for four days while struggling through the balance of reasoning and God's provision: the resurrection of Maria from the ashes.

Regarding waiting longer, giving more time to observe before sharing the news of what God has done, I began feeling like the lepers in 2 Kings. I can see the miracle in front of me and must share.

Then Elisha said, Hear ye the word of the Lord; Thus saith the Lord, To morrow about this time shall a measure of fine flour be sold for a shekel, and two measures of barley for a shekel, in the gate of Samaria... Then they said one to another, We do not well: this day is a day of good tidings, and we hold our peace: if we tarry till the morning light, some mischief will come upon us: now therefore come, that we may go and tell the king's household.

—2 Kings 7:1,9

This is the first time she has been whole since March 2021, and God has taken away her sickness just as suddenly as it appeared.

She is completely in her right mind with full recollection of all that has happened.

Our friends rejoiced with us, and the days that followed were filled with a deep sense of gratitude. My heart overflowed with thanksgiving and a renewed sense of responsibility. God had restored me for a purpose.

No Longer Bound

I felt unmistakable joy and liberty after being set free from the grip of anxiety and depression. Before that moment, each day dawned with dread. I had trouble talking to people because fear would constrict my throat. But now, every day began with promise. Love had replaced fear, making room for meaningful conversations.

The realization that I was no longer bound by irrational beliefs lifted a heavy burden. The paralyzing anxiety that had held me captive was gone. I had avoided food, worried about contamination, and even kept my distance from people. The list felt endless. I questioned everyone and everything. But after that moment of surrender, clarity returned. I trusted my husband, I enjoyed our pets, and I knew my meals were safe. I could eat with confidence.

The next time we went out to eat, I realized I didn't have to order my meal without spices. The allergies I thought I had were imagined. Taking in all the sights and sounds of my surroundings and relishing the companionship of my husband was just the beginning.

Something else changed. Without even knowing it, I had carried mistrust all my life. I approached relationships with a sense of insecurity, and I longed for the approval of others. Mistrust affected all my relationships, including those with my husband, family, friends, and even my relationship with God.

After my healing, I no longer felt the need to hide my past or the messiness of my journey through anxiety and depression. It was as if a barrier that had once blocked full communion with my Heavenly Father had been removed. For the first time, our relationship felt complete.

That wholeness began to overflow into all my other relationships, especially my marriage. With a deep sense of freedom, I shared this revelation with my husband, Steve: "*I don't have anything to hide.*"

Our first conversation after my healing was like diving into a crystal-clear mountain stream after a grueling uphill climb. It was refreshing and altogether invigorating. Sharing openly about our experiences and exploring the reasons behind them invited God's healing process to continue. It was not the end of the journey; it was the beginning of learning how to walk in freedom.

Staying Proactive

Steve and I both understood the importance of staying proactive and diligent after God's miraculous gift of healing. We knew the enemy would be on the prowl, using his cunning strategies and deceitful tactics to lure me back into bondage.

Little by little, the Lord helped my husband discern that childhood trauma had shaped my response to conflict. Freezing, or becoming stuck, had become my default: an ingrained reaction that bred mistrust. Over time, the suppression of my thoughts and feelings erupted in defensive outbursts, when I reacted sharply to perceived threats in a desperate attempt to protect myself.

A few weeks later, when a disagreement arose, I found myself lashing out with irrational statements, falling back into an all-too-familiar pattern. Steve noticed the behavior for what it was and gently pointed out the survival mode reaction. He was right. Within minutes of the argument, the tension began to drain from my body, and I could breathe again.

The more wisdom the Lord gave us, the more I became aware of how trauma influenced my decision-making. With my husband's help, I began identifying triggers and working through the issues, step by step, to change my behavior. It's an ongoing journey, one I'm still learning to navigate.

Like the Psalmist David, I asked the Lord to show me things I needed to change:

"Search me, O God, and know my heart: try me, and know my thoughts: And see if there be any wicked way in me, and lead me in the way everlasting" (Psalm 139:23–24).

I asked forgiveness for attempting to end my life. Instead of wearing guilt like a garment, I rested in my Father's righteousness. It was true: His grace was greater than my sin; I was forgiven.

Moving Forward

Moving forward in humility was important. It required me to recognize and acknowledge my limitations and weaknesses. Just a few weeks earlier, I had avoided reading God's Word. Now, my hope was ignited, and His Word seemed to come alive. I was overwhelmed by the depth of His love. More than just a fleeting feeling, it was written unmistakably on every page of Scripture.

Worship overflowed during my time with the Lord as the opening lines of this joyful psalm came alive:

I will bless the Lord at all times: his praise shall continually be in my mouth.

My soul shall make her boast in the Lord: the humble shall hear thereof, and be glad.

O magnify the Lord with me, and let us exalt his name together.

I sought the Lord, and he heard me, and delivered me from all my fears.

—Psalm 34:1–4

Talking to my Heavenly Father was precious. It felt easier to share painful emotions with Him now, and He was healing me at a deeper level. As I read and studied His Word and spent time with Him in prayer, I discovered more of God's character. The harsh, judgmental God I imagined during psychosis was nowhere to be found. Through a lens of liberty, I now saw Him as loving, kind, compassionate, just, holy, merciful, patient, and forgiving. His desire, as it had always been, was to have a close and intimate relationship with me.

The trial of anxiety and depression was never meant to overpower me. Like the loving Master Potter He is, the Lord used it to mold and shape me into His image, forming a vessel ready to be poured out in service to others. In the days ahead, I would begin to see exactly what that looked like.

Help and Hope from God's Word

There's no doubt, we are engaged in a spiritual battle. The good news is that the Lord has equipped us with everything we need to be victorious, giving us both the armor for the conflict and a plan to help us avoid the enemy's traps: "Finally, my brethren, be strong in the Lord, and in the power of his might. Put on the whole armour of God, that ye may be able to stand against the wiles of the devil" (Ephesians 6:10–11).

I'm so thankful we don't have to face anxiety and depression in our own strength. We can stand firm in the Lord's strength and power. And have you noticed the "designer label" on our protective gear? It bears the name of Almighty God: complete, powerful, and able to withstand anything the enemy throws our way.

Looking back, I see how costly it was to fight without that protection. I hadn't consciously "put on" the armor of God. My mind was overrun with fear, my heart was weighed down with guilt and shame, and my spirit was exposed to every attack.

After the Lord brought victory, the intensity of the battle came into focus. I could see how the enemy had used lies, condemnation, fear, and doubt to keep me bound. Now I know I can't let my guard down. The enemy will look for every possible way to pull me back into captivity. I must be prepared for what lies ahead.

Our Mighty Armor

Each day, I deliberately put on the protection He provides. It's not a ritual; it's a vital safeguard for my mind and spirit. Each morning, I picture fastening the belt of truth around my waist, securing the helmet of salvation on my head, and gripping the sword of the Spirit firmly in my hand. I know each piece has a purpose. Without them, I'm far more vulnerable than I ever want to be again.

The apostle Paul outlines our spiritual battle gear in Ephesians 6. Each piece is God-given and perfectly crafted for the spiritual skirmishes we face.

Belt of truth (Ephesians 6:14)

A Roman soldier's leather belt secured the rest of his armor. The King James Study Bible explains, "...the other pieces of the Christian's armor depend on, and are held in place by, his spiritual 'belt' or his knowledge of the 'truth' of Scripture."[1]

During my battle, lies often went unchecked: *You don't measure up. God is angry with you. You've gone too far to ever be free.* These thoughts brought me down and directly attacked my identity in Christ.

To remain free from anxiety's grasp today, I can put on the belt of truth each morning, measuring every thought against Scripture. When I hold up a lie against verses like Psalm 139:14a—"I am fearfully and wonderfully made"—it crumbles.

Breastplate of righteousness (Ephesians 6:14)

This piece guards the heart, representing "a holy character and moral conduct."[2] Living out the truth we've been given produces a godly life.

When I was weighed down with depression, guilt struck a heavy blow. I believed God could never forgive me for attempting suicide, thinking I was disqualified from being His child or serving Him. Without the breastplate, each strike went straight to my heart.

Now, as I clothe myself in God's breastplate, my heart is covered—not by my own performance, but by Christ's righteousness, which shields me from shame before it can pierce me.

Shoes of the gospel of peace (Ephesians 6:15)

Roman soldiers wore *caligae*, a type of specialized sandal that provided them with stability and traction to advance against their enemies.[3] Without them, forward movement was impossible.

In my lowest moments, I stayed "holed up" where fear told me it was safe. I isolated myself from people, places, and even opportunities God might have used to help me walk in freedom.

Wearing these supernatural shoes of peace, I'm reminded I can step forward with confidence, whether entering a hard conversation, showing up for ministry, or caring for my husband's needs. I carry peace because Christ lives in me, and His presence is greater than the enemy's threats (1 John 4:4).

Shield of faith (Ephesians 6:16)

Roman shields were often wooden, "covered with leather and soaked in water before the battle."[4] When a fiery dart struck, the wet leather extinguished the flames.

During my trial, I stood unprotected, an easy target for the enemy's burning arrows of fear, doubt, and condemnation. My faith was so weak that I couldn't lift the shield in defense.

Now I'm keenly aware of the fight, quick to recognize these attacks for what they are: temptations designed to take me down. When fear whispers, *You're not safe*, I counter with Psalm 56:3: "What time I am afraid, I will trust in thee." The shield of faith quenches every dart.

Helmet of salvation (Ephesians 6:17)

The helmet protects the mind, not to save us again, but to guard us with the certainty of our salvation.

When depression clouded my thoughts, I began to doubt my salvation, convinced my failures had somehow canceled it. I forgot the truth that nothing could separate me from the love of God (Romans 8:38–39) and instead imagined He was distant and angry. Without the helmet, those lies slipped in easily. Soon, I found myself trapped in a web of deception with no way out.

Today, I know my helmet must be firmly in place. It reminds me: *My salvation is secure. I am a child of God.* I belong to Him, not because of how I feel, but because of what Christ has done. This certainty guards my mind from spiraling into fear or striving to earn His approval.

Sword of the Spirit (Ephesians 6:17)

Our only offensive weapon is God's Word. In battle, a soldier doesn't wait until the attack to learn how to use his sword. He trains with it daily.

After recovering from anxiety in 2006, I gradually stopped swinging my sword, mistakenly believing I no longer needed to be vigilant. So when fear returned, I wasn't ready to wield Scripture. Recognizing our weaknesses helps us identify the Bible passages we'll need for the fight.

I now keep God's Word close, storing truth in my heart that directly counters the enemy's attacks. One of my go-to weapons is Isaiah 26:3: "Thou wilt keep him in perfect peace, whose mind is stayed on thee: because he trusteth in thee." Declaring it slowly while breathing deeply centers my focus on the Lord, effectively slicing through the enemy's lies.

Five of the pieces of armor are defensive in nature. They shield and protect. But the sword of the Spirit, paired with prayer, puts us on the offensive. I've learned that none of this armor is optional. It's the difference between standing firm and being taken down. Facing anxiety and depression without protection is a mistake I will not repeat. The cost is too great.

God has provided armor that is battle-tested and sure. All that's left is to suit up prayerfully and step forward, fully armed. Protection is essential, and He's given us a clear strategy for the fight: steps to take when the enemy presses in.

Our Strategy for Victory

Each skirmish with anxiety and depression may look different, but God has given us a clear path to avoid the enemy's traps. Much of it is found in the book of James, with insights from other Scriptures:

Search your heart: Desire truth in the deepest parts of your being. Ask God to reveal the root cause behind what you're thinking and feeling, trusting that He will set you free.

> "Behold, thou desirest truth in the inward parts: and in the hidden part thou shalt make me to know wisdom" (Psalm 51:6).

Stay humble in spirit: Confess any sin to God and seek forgiveness from those you've wronged. Humility opens the door to God's grace.

"But he giveth more grace. Wherefore he saith, God resisteth the proud, but giveth grace unto the humble" (James 4:6).

Submit your will to God: Surrender your will to His, remembering that trials shape you to be more like Christ.

"Submit yourself therefore to God" (James 4:7a).

Resist the devil: Be alert to his schemes. He will target your weakest points. Stand firm in the authority of Christ.

"Resist the devil, and he will flee from you" (James 4:7b).

Draw near to God: Pursue Him through Scripture and prayer. Pour out your heart and listen for His voice. He desires a close relationship with you.

"Draw nigh to God, and he will draw nigh to you" (James 4:8a).

Reach out to others: Surround yourself with friends who seek Christ and will speak truth into your life.

"Iron sharpeneth iron; so a man sharpeneth the countenance of his friend" (Proverbs 27:17).

Share your struggles: Be honest about the areas where you need help. Invite others to pray with and for you.

"Confess your faults one to another, and pray one for another, that ye may be healed. The effectual fervent prayer of a righteous man availeth much" (James 5:16).

Praise the Lord: In every season, whether you are entering a trial, walking through one, or coming out on the other side, worship God with a grateful heart.

"Rejoice evermore. Pray without ceasing. In every thing give thanks: for this is the will of God in Christ Jesus concerning you" (1 Thessalonians 5:16–18).

Our Savior never promised the journey would be easy, but He walks with you through every trial. With His armor in place, stand firm. Guard your heart. Fix your eyes on Him. Step forward in faith. Your victory is certain. One battle at a time.

 Your Turn: Reflection Questions and Action Steps

Pause and Reflect

1. How do mistrust and insecurity affect your relationship with God and with others?

2. What past wounds or experiences might still influence your thoughts, emotions, or reactions today?

3. Can you recall a moment when you felt God's presence strongly? How did it change your outlook?

4. How are you preparing spiritually each day to face the challenges of anxiety and depression?

5. Which piece of God's armor do you most often neglect to "put on," and how has that left you vulnerable in your spiritual battles?

6. How has sharing your struggles with others impacted your faith and healing?

7. How does practicing gratitude and praise shape your perspective during trials?

Live It Out

1. **Surrender to God:** Release one area of control to Him and pray over it daily.

2. **Heal from the past:** Pinpoint moments that spark unhealthy responses and invite a trusted advisor or counselor to walk with you in healing.

3. **Practice humility and confession:** Confess known sin to God and seek forgiveness from those you've wronged.

4. **Suit up daily:** Begin each morning in prayer, intentionally putting on each piece of armor: fastening the belt, securing the helmet, lifting the shield, and taking up the sword.

5. **Identify your weak spots:** Reflect on your recent struggles and note which lies or fears you most often believe. Find Scripture that directly counters each one and keep those verses where you can see them daily.

6. **Stay resilient:** Choose one practical step from James 4 to avoid the traps of anxiety and depression.

7. **Maintain gratitude:** Thank God for His provision, protection, and one specific blessing that He has given you today.

Can I Pray for You?

Heavenly Father, You are aware of the spiritual battle we face. Thank You for giving us both the armor and the plan we need to walk in victory. As we get ready each morning, remind us to prepare our hearts by fastening the belt of truth—Your Word. Guard us with the breastplate of righteousness, leading us toward holiness. Help us advance with confidence, knowing Your gospel brings peace that frees us from the grip of anxiety. Though our enemy is powerful, he cannot stand against us when we walk in the strength of Your peace. Strengthen us to lift the shield of faith, trusting that it will quench every fiery dart the enemy launches our way. Protect our minds with the helmet of salvation, keeping us secure in the assurance of Christ's sacrifice. Teach us to wield the sword of the Spirit effectively, answering every lie with the power of Your Word. We want Your truth to reign in us. Keep us diligent and aware of anything that trips us up. Lead us to humility, and prompt us to confess any sin You reveal. Lord, we choose Your will over our own. Your Word says our adversary is like a roaring lion, seeking someone to devour. Strengthen us to stand firm and resist his schemes. Draw us closer to You and deepen our understanding of who You are. Surround us with believers who will encourage and sharpen us. Give us the courage to be honest and vulnerable with one another. We choose to rejoice and give thanks, for You are good and faithful. And You walk with us every step of the way. In Jesus' name, Amen.

Works Cited

[1] *The King James Study Bible: Full Color Edition.* Thomas Nelson, 2017, p. 1895.

[2] *The King James Study Bible: Full Color Edition.* Thomas Nelson, 2017, p. 1895.

[3] Raison, Daniel. "Roman Soldier Shoes: All the Curiosities." *Res Militares*, 27 Jan. 2025, https://resmilitares.com/en/roman-soldier-shoes/. Accessed 8 Aug. 2025.

[4] Srock, Jonathan. "3 Powers of the Shield of Faith." *Jonathan Srock*, 12 Nov. 2021, https://jonathansrock.com/3-powers-of-the-shield-of-faith/. Accessed 8 Aug. 2025.

10

Use Your Story for His Glory

My Life Lesson

God set me free from my two-and-a-half-year battle with fear and darkness, and I couldn't keep silent. Gratitude overflowed as I reconnected with family and friends, eager to share the long, hard journey that ended in His miraculous healing.

One afternoon, I met a long-time friend for lunch, a friend who had prayed for me faithfully through the darkest days. The clatter of dishes and low hum of conversation surrounded us as we stood in line. That's when I spotted my former therapist ahead of us, waiting for her meal. We exchanged a quick embrace, and I whispered, *"I'm healed."* Her wide eyes and vigorous nod said it all. The transformation was undeniable to both of us.

Minutes later, my friend and I settled into a corner table. She leaned in, her smile warm with relief, and said how thankful she was to see me whole again. Emotion caught in my throat as I recounted how God had lifted the weight and restored my mind.

As I continued to share my story with others, I discovered that I wasn't alone. Many Christians had battled anxiety, depression, psychosis, and even thoughts of suicide. The enemy's whisper that my struggle was unique was nothing but a lie. Bringing everything into the open and exposing it to the light stripped it of its power. Truth prevailed: God's healing in my life could be the spark that ignited hope in someone else.

Undeniable Transformation

Only days after my healing, I walked into my psychologist's office. She was visibly stunned. The difference between the woman who initially came to her for help and the one who stood before her now was unmistakable. The empty stare was gone, replaced by a calm radiance. She listened carefully as I recounted what transpired.

What she said next caught me off guard. Her voice carried disbelief as she explained that full recovery from the level of psychosis I had experienced was very rare. Most people battling psychosis required inpatient treatment, and the clients she had seen with severe paranoia had all abruptly ended therapy sessions, unable to recognize their thinking as irrational.

Her surprise made me wonder if others might question my healing, or even feel frustrated that I had received a miracle when they had not. Sometimes the painful situation remains, yet God gives additional measures of grace to bear up under the trial. He is close to the brokenhearted and walks with us through every valley. His plan is unique for each of us, and His Word reminds us that He is able to do the impossible. Miracles still happen in His perfect timing—there is always hope.

That day, a deep sense of humility was born in my heart. Gratitude welled up as I realized I had done nothing to deserve this healing. It was a precious gift: an unmistakable expression of God's mercy that pointed beyond me to a loving Heavenly Father.

Growth Continues

At our next session, I asked her why I still tended to shut down or change the subject whenever conflict arose, even after all these years. Her answer filled in the blanks. As a child, I had discovered that withdrawing or deflecting kept me safe during conflict. My nervous system, designed by God to protect me, recorded those strategies as "safety plans," which became automatic responses. Decades later, even when I was safe, my body still reacted as though the old threat remained.

We also reviewed the practices that were helping me walk forward in freedom: reading God's Word, praying, reconnecting with friends, communicating honestly, and staying accountable. She nodded, affirming the importance of each one.

Looking ahead, she encouraged me to develop healthier ways of responding to conflict. No further sessions were necessary unless I had more questions or new challenges arose.

When I met with my psychiatrist soon afterward, her response mirrored my psychologist's: amazement at the transformation that had taken place. Together, we discussed a careful plan to begin tapering off my prescription medication. Under her guidance, and with the support of my holistic doctor, I transitioned off the medication over nine months, replacing it with natural supplements that strengthened my system.

As I ate healthy meals, took supplements, started exercising, and got much-needed sleep, my body began to heal. I also learned how the nervous system itself could be rewired. Neuropsychologist, Dr. Michelle Bengtson, explains it this way, "The good news is that just as childhood trauma shapes how we cope as adults, healing from trauma can transform the way we handle future challenges. It's never too late to rewrite the narrative of how we respond to adversity. The first step in healing from childhood trauma is recognizing that it exists and that it has an impact on our present-day responses."[1]

Her words beautifully captured what I was experiencing: just as God had restored my mind, He was renewing the very patterns of how I responded to life.

Guarding the Ground You've Gained

The Lord gave me victory over anxiety and depression, but that didn't mean I would never face stress or conflict again. On this side of heaven, tension will always be a part of life. At times, I've slipped back into familiar negative thought patterns, and it often shows in how I speak or respond to others.

During those moments, Steve gently points them out and encourages me to view things from a different perspective. Sometimes that means asking myself: *What is true in this situation? Am I assuming the worst? Have I prayed about this yet?* Other times, it means pausing to take a deep breath, reminding myself I'm safe, and replacing the anxious thought with a Scripture verse I've memorized.

The weekly accountability sessions with friends, following the *Day of Truth,* have continued and proven invaluable. They are sacred times of prayer. Safe spaces to voice struggles. When I've battled comparison or begun relying on myself instead of the Lord, I confess it. Yet, I remain confident that He is continuing the work He began in me (Philippians 1:6).

With the support of my husband and others, I can put these tools into practice and overcome the inner struggle. Consciously addressing these issues is soul work that continues to this day.

Passing On the Comfort

The comfort I received wasn't meant for me alone; it was also intended to be shared with others. The first time my husband and I shared our testimony at church, the response was overwhelming. I gave voice to the guilt and shame that had caused me to isolate and keep silent for so long. I acknowledged the need for humility within the local church: the willingness to confess our weaknesses to one another and ask for prayer in order to experience victory.

Men and women of all ages, from teens to older adults, resonated with our message. The need to be open and honest about the struggle—from both the sufferer's and caregiver's perspectives—was crucial. This was the moment the Lord began confirming my desire to share with others the same wisdom, help, and hope He had graciously poured into me.

It was no surprise when the Lord began bringing people into my life who were battling anxiety and depression. While each person's story was unique, many shared a common thread: early trauma that the enemy continued to use to trap them in a cycle of defeat. Though the devil's plan has always been to steal, kill, and destroy, Jesus came to offer each of us abundant life (John 10:10).

The Beauty of Trials

The Lord allows us to face trials for many reasons. Wherever you are on your journey, I understand the refining process is hard. Remember that God is with you and is on your side. Even your current struggle with anxiety or depression can be used for a greater purpose.

Sometimes, it takes a difficult season to shape us to look more like Jesus. The apostle Paul reminds us:

> And we know that all things work together for good to them that love God, to them who are the called according to his purpose. For whom he did foreknow, he also did predestinate to be conformed to the image of his Son, that he might be the firstborn among many brethren.
>
> —Romans 8:28–29

Other times, the hardships and seasons of loss we experience can bring renewal and hope. The prophet Joel gave God's hope-filled promise, "And I will restore to you the years that the locust hath eaten. . ." (Joel 2:25).

When we emerge from a trial, we can look back and recognize the hand of our Heavenly Father who brought us safely through. Along the way, His steady hand gives comfort, and He entrusts us with the privilege of extending that same comfort to others. Paul's words assure us: "Blessed be God, even the Father of our Lord Jesus Christ, the Father of mercies, and the God of all comfort; Who comforteth us in all our tribulation, that we may be able to comfort them which are in any trouble, by the comfort wherewith we ourselves are comforted of God" (2 Corinthians 1:3–4).

I am grateful our Heavenly Father is continually at work, conforming us into His image—chiseling away what doesn't belong and refining the rough edges. When anxiety attacks or depression presses in, we can meet these trials with truth. We can fight back with joy and hope, trusting that the outcome God has planned will be beautiful.

Help and Hope from God's Word

Did you know some of the greatest men in the Bible faced times of anxiety and despair? The prophet Elijah was no exception. He encountered a significant trial that left him grappling with intense apprehension and hopelessness. But how did he get to that place?

Elijah was a man of God who boldly confronted King Ahab, declaring there would be no dew or rain in Israel until he gave the word. That may sound harsh, but a closer look at Ahab's character provides context: "And Ahab made a grove; and Ahab did more to provoke the Lord God of Israel to anger than all the kings of Israel that were before him" (1 Kings 16:33). He led the people astray and encouraged them to worship false gods.

Following three years of drought, the Lord sent Elijah to rebuke the king. Elijah had Ahab summon all the people of Israel, along with the prophets of Baal and the prophets of the groves, to Mount Carmel. When everyone was assembled, Elijah asked a pivotal question, "…How long halt ye between two opinions? if the Lord be God, follow him: but if Baal, then follow him. And the people answered him not a word" (1 Kings 18:21). The people were silent.

The Contest

The stillness was broken by Elijah's proposal: a contest to determine the true God. The false prophets would prepare a sacrifice and call on their gods, while Elijah would prepare a sacrifice and call on the name of the Lord. The God who answered with fire would be declared the one true God.

From morning until evening, the false prophets cried out in desperation to their gods, but no answer came. When it was Elijah's turn, he repaired the altar of the Lord with twelve stones, dug a trench around it, and placed wood and a sacrifice on top. Then, in an unexpected move, he had the people pour water over the altar—not once, but three times—until it drenched the sacrifice and filled the trench.

With everything saturated, Elijah prayed: "Lord God of Abraham, Isaac, and of Israel, let it be known this day that thou art God in Israel, and that I am thy servant, and that I have done all these things at thy word. Hear me, O Lord, hear me, that this people may know that thou art the Lord

God, and that thou hast turned their heart back again" (1 Kings 18:36b–37).

Immediately, the Lord sent fire that consumed the sacrifice, the wood, the stones, and even the water. Elijah and all the people witnessed God's incredible power on Mount Carmel that day. The people fell on their faces, acknowledging the Lord as the one true God, and obeyed Elijah's command to put the false prophets to death.

The Valley of Despair

It was an incredible mountaintop experience. But, as often happens, the mountaintop was followed by a deep valley. When Jezebel, King Ahab's wife, learned the prophets were dead, she was furious. She sent Elijah a death threat: "...So let the gods do to me, and more also, if I make not thy life as the life of one of them by to morrow about this time" (1 Kings 19:2).

Elijah had just witnessed God's mighty power, yet fear overwhelmed him. He fled for his life, left his servant in Beersheba, and traveled alone into the wilderness. Exhausted, he sat under a juniper tree and made a heartfelt plea, ". . . It is enough; now, O Lord, take away my life; for I am not better than my fathers" (1 Kings 19:4). Even God's prophet reached a point of despair, longing for his life to end.

But the Lord didn't rebuke or criticize Elijah. He understood Elijah's physical and emotional exhaustion and sent an angel with food and water, providing him with rest. God met him right where he was and tenderly provided for his needs. Twice, Elijah ate, drank, and slept. Strengthened, he traveled forty days to Mount Horeb.

Even after God's provision, Elijah's despair lingered: "And he said, I have been very jealous for the Lord God of hosts: for the children of Israel have forsaken thy covenant, thrown down thine altars, and slain thy prophets with the sword; and I, even I only, am left; and they seek my life, to take it away" (1 Kings 19:10).

Do you sense Elijah's discouragement? He was convinced he was the only prophet still faithfully serving God. Then, God revealed His presence. Not in a mighty wind, a powerful earthquake, or a consuming fire—but in a still small voice. He repeated the question, "What doest thou here, Elijah?" (1 Kings 19:13b).

Again, Elijah repeated his lament (v. 14). Yet instead of chastising him, God reassured Elijah that he was not alone. There were 7,000 others who had remained faithful. God recommissioned him, giving him new tasks and a successor, Elisha.

God's Gentle Care

God was faithful to meet all of Elijah's needs during his valley experience:

- **Body:** The Lord supplied food, water, and rest.
- **Soul:** The Lord renewed his purpose and reminded him of others who would continue the ministry.
- **Spirit:** The Lord assured him of His presence throughout the intense struggle.

Elijah had become so focused on his problem that he lost sight of God's purpose and plan. Does that sound familiar to you?

When battling anxiety or depression, our focus narrows until we miss God's presence and the greater story He is writing. The same God who strengthened Elijah longs to strengthen you: body, soul, and spirit.

God's ultimate desire is for you to look more like Him and reflect Him to those around you. Your difficult story can be transformed into one of hope—a story that encourages others and brings great glory to Him.

 Your Turn: Reflection Questions and Action Steps

Pause and Reflect

1. What truths have strengthened you in your battle with anxiety and depression?

2. When old thought patterns resurface, how do you confront them with God's truth?

3. How has your awareness of God's presence changed throughout your journey?

4. Why is a supportive community vital when you face anxiety or depression?

5. How does God's gentle care for Elijah encourage you in your walk with Him?

6. Where can you shift your focus from problems to God's presence and plan?

7. What new tasks or purposes might God be inviting you to step into, even in the middle of your struggle?

Live It Out

1. **Seek God's healing:** Identify one area of your life in need of His touch, and pray for His transforming power.

2. **Break the silence:** Share honestly with a trusted friend or family member about both your struggles and victories, resisting the pull to isolate.

3. **Rest in His presence:** Set aside time with God, allowing His comfort to fill your heart and mind.

4. **Learn from Scripture:** Read another biblical story of someone who faced trials and overcame with God's help.

5. **Record His faithfulness:** Keep a journal of answered prayers to remind yourself of God's goodness.

6. **Embrace God's call:** Stay open to God's recommissioning. Watch for new tasks, purposes, or missions He may place on your heart.

7. **Serve with hope:** Encourage someone facing a similar struggle. As you serve, notice how God fills your heart with hope.

Can I Pray for You?

Heavenly Father, Your love is beyond our comprehension. You long to have fellowship and walk with us each day, whether on the mountaintop or in the deepest valley. We confess how easily doubt and despair slip in when trials come. Guard our hearts and minds with Your perspective. Remind us of the victories You've already given. Give us grace to invite others into our struggles and courage to bear one another's burdens instead of seeking isolation. Thank You for faithfully meeting our needs: body, soul, and spirit. We praise You for daily provision—for food, water, shelter, and rest. Thank You for surrounding us with friends and family who encourage and support us. What a privilege it is to experience Your presence. Help us shift our gaze from our problems to You and Your greater vision. Equip us to embrace the tasks and purposes You set before us. Make us more like You. Bring renewal and hope after our trials. Encourage us to comfort others with the comfort You've given us. As we depend on You, fill us with freedom, joy, and purpose so we can live out our calling in You, all for Your glory. In the mighty name of Jesus, Amen.

Works Cited

[1] Bengtson, Michelle. "Healing from Childhood Trauma: How It Affects Our Adult Responses." *Dr. Michelle Bengtson*, 11 June 2025, https://drmichellebengtson.com/healing-from-childhood-trauma/. Accessed 18 Aug. 2025.

Afterword

*L*ooking back on the desert season that culminated in writing this book, I'm in awe of the goodness of God. He pursued me as I grappled with anxiety and depression, and I'm certain He will walk with me no matter what lies ahead. Healing wasn't the end of the journey—it was the breaking of chains that once kept me bound. It was an invitation to renew my trust in God and to move forward in surrender.

Will there be days when old thought patterns resurface? Absolutely. Fear will still whisper its familiar lies, trying to pull me back into bondage. But I don't fight alone. The enemy wages war on every part of who I am (body, soul, and spirit), and remembering that truth keeps me alert. Caring for my body, leaning on godly friends, putting on God's armor, and running to Him with every anxious thought: these anchor me to the One who is my strength.

Your story may not mirror mine. Healing doesn't always come instantly. Sometimes it unfolds gradually, and at times God allows ongoing treatment to remain part of the process. That doesn't make your story any less valuable or miraculous. Jesus walks faithfully with you every step of the way, whether your pace is fast or slow, your healing complete or still ongoing.

Trust God to take every piece—no matter how broken, mismatched, or messy—and weave them into something beautiful for your good and His glory. The enemy will try to convince you there's no hope, that you're disqualified. But the opposite is true: God delights in you, and He will use the trials you've endured to kindle hope in someone else.

Just as He pursued me in my darkest valley, He is pursuing you. Will you take a step of faith today? Even the smallest steps matter. Stay connected to Jesus as your Source by renewing your trust in Him. Perhaps He's prompting you to share your own story as He gives you the opportunity. Whatever He calls you to do, follow His leading with open hands, a willing spirit, and a surrendered heart.

It's been a privilege to walk with you through these pages. My prayer is that the truths and tools you've discovered will help you renew your mind, strengthen your faith, and embrace freedom, joy, and purpose in who you are in Christ—one day at a time.

"Now unto him that is able to do exceeding abundantly above all that we ask or think, according to the power that worketh in us, Unto him be glory in the church by Christ Jesus throughout all ages, world without end. Amen" (Ephesians 3:20–21).

Appendix A
Understanding the Terms

Anxiety: According to Mayo Clinic, anxiety is "intense, excessive, and prolonged worry and fear about everyday situations. People with anxiety disorders frequently have repeated episodes of sudden feelings of intense anxiety and fear or terror that reach a peak within minutes (panic attacks)."[1]

Depression: Mayo Clinic defines depression (major depressive disorder) as "a mood disorder that causes a persistent feeling of sadness and loss of interest. It affects how you feel, think, and behave and can lead to a variety of emotional and physical problems."[2]

Psychosis: The National Institute of Mental Health (NIMH) describes psychosis as:

> A collection of symptoms that affect the mind, where there has been some loss of contact with reality. During an episode of psychosis, a person's thoughts and perceptions are disrupted and they may have difficulty recognizing what is real and what is not. . . . People with

psychosis typically experience delusions (false beliefs, for example, that people on television are sending them special messages or that others are trying to hurt them) and hallucinations (seeing or hearing things that others do not, such as hearing voices telling them to do something or criticizing them). Other symptoms can include incoherent or nonsense speech and behavior that is inappropriate for the situation.[3]

Works Cited

[1]   Mayo Clinic. "Anxiety Disorders." *Mayo Clinic*, 4 Dec. 2023, https://www.mayoclinic.org/diseases-conditions/anxiety/symptoms-causes/syc-20350961. Accessed 25 Aug. 2025.

[2]   Mayo Clinic. "Depression (Major Depressive Disorder)." *Mayo Clinic*, 3 Feb. 2024, https://www.mayoclinic.org/diseases-conditions/depression/symptoms-causes/syc-20356007. Accessed 25 Aug. 2025.

[3]   National Institute of Mental Health. *Understanding Psychosis*. U.S. Department of Health and Human Services, 2024, https://www.nimh.nih.gov/health/publications/understanding-psychosis. Accessed 25 Aug. 2025.

Appendix B

An Invitation to Know Jesus

*I*f you don't have a relationship with Jesus Christ, I'd love to introduce you to Him. When sin entered the world through Adam and Eve, it broke humanity's fellowship with a holy God. A payment was required to restore the relationship. God sent His Son, Jesus—the perfect, sinless sacrifice—to die on the cross as the full payment for sin: past, present, and future. He was buried and rose again three days later. The debt for our sins was paid in full, and the gift of salvation is now offered to us.

Salvation is by grace alone, through faith alone, in Christ alone. God invites us to have a relationship with Him. When we repent of our sins, believe in Jesus' death, burial, and resurrection, and accept His gift of salvation by faith, God forgives us, makes us His children, and gives us eternal life.

He's extending this invitation today. Consider some verses that clearly demonstrate His love for you:

Recognize Your Need

We have all sinned and fallen short of God's standard.

> "For all have sinned, and come short of the glory of God" (Romans 3:23).

> "All we like sheep have gone astray; we have turned every one to his own way; and the Lord hath laid on him the iniquity of us all" (Isaiah 53:6).

Understand Sin's Consequences

Sin carries a penalty we cannot escape.

> "For the wages of sin is death; but the gift of God is eternal life through Jesus Christ our Lord" (Romans 6:23).

> "And as it is appointed unto men once to die, but after this the judgment" (Hebrews 9:27).

Believe God's Provision

God showed His love by sending Jesus Christ to pay our debt.

> "But God commendeth his love toward us, in that, while we were yet sinners, Christ died for us" (Romans 5:8).

> "For God so loved the world, that he gave his only begotten Son, that whosoever believeth in him should not perish, but have everlasting life" (John 3:16).

Accept His Gift by Faith

Salvation is free. We receive it by faith, not works.

> "For by grace are ye saved through faith; and that not of yourselves: it is the gift of God: Not of works, lest any man should boast" (Ephesians 2:8–9).

"Knowing that a man is not justified by the works of the law, but by the faith of Jesus Christ, even we have believed in Jesus Christ, that we might be justified by the faith of Christ, and not by the works of the law: for by the works of the law shall no flesh be justified" (Galatians 2:16).

Confess and Trust Christ

To receive salvation, we must believe in our hearts and confess Christ as Lord.

"That if thou shalt confess with thy mouth the Lord Jesus, and shalt believe in thine heart that God hath raised him from the dead, thou shalt be saved. For with the heart man believeth unto righteousness; and with the mouth confession is made unto salvation" (Romans 10:9–10).

"For whosoever shall call upon the name of the Lord shall be saved" (Romans 10:13).

Did you receive God's gift of salvation by faith today? If so, I rejoice with you! I'd love to encourage you as you begin your new walk with Him.

Appendix C
God's Character

Omnipotent (All-Powerful)

"For with God nothing shall be impossible" (Luke 1:37).

Omniscient (All-Knowing)

"Great is our Lord, and of great power: his understanding is infinite" (Psalm 147:5).

Holy (Pure and Righteous)

"Who is like unto thee, O Lord, among the gods? who is like thee, glorious in holiness, fearful in praises, doing wonders?" (Exodus 15:11).

Loving (Characterized by Love)

"He that loveth not knoweth not God; for God is love" (1 John 4:8).

Just (Fair)

"He is the Rock, his work is perfect: for all his ways are judgment: a God of truth and without iniquity, just and right is he" (Deuteronomy 32:4).

Merciful (Showing Compassion and Forgiveness)

"But God, who is rich in mercy, for his great love wherewith he loved us" (Ephesians 2:4).

Faithful (Reliable and Trustworthy)

"Know therefore that the Lord thy God, he is God, the faithful God, which keepeth covenant and mercy with them that love him and keep his commandments to a thousand generations" (Deuteronomy 7:9).

He is all these things and infinitely more. Meditate on each of these characteristics and respond as the Lord leads.

Appendix D
Our Identity in Christ

Blessed

"Blessed be the God and Father of our Lord Jesus Christ, who hath blessed us with all spiritual blessings in heavenly places in Christ" (Ephesians 1:3).

Chosen

"According as he hath chosen us in him before the foundation of the world, that we should be holy and without blame before him in love" (Ephesians 1:4).

Adopted

"Having predestinated us unto the adoption of children by Jesus Christ to himself, according to the good pleasure of his will" (Ephesians 1:5).

Redeemed and Forgiven

"In whom we have redemption through his blood, the forgiveness of sins, according to the riches of his grace" (Ephesians 1:7).

Sealed with the Holy Spirit

"In whom ye also trusted, after that ye heard the word of truth, the gospel of your salvation: in whom also after that ye believed, ye were sealed with that holy Spirit of promise" (Ephesians 1:13).

Holy

"But as he which hath called you is holy, so be ye holy in all manner of conversation; Because it is written, Be ye holy: for I am holy" (1 Peter 1:15–16).

Victorious

"For whatsoever is born of God overcometh the world: and this is the victory that overcometh the world, even our faith" (1 John 5:4).

This is who we are. Embrace your identity as His child.